"What a liberating resource! Just reading the first paragraph will set you free. But don't stop there. Every chapter is full of honest insights into how the gospel can change both you and the way you parent."

Charles Morris, Speaker and President of the nationwide radio broadcast *Haven Today*

"If I'm honest, too often my parenting has a 'build-a-better-Pharisee' feel to it— I'm sadly content to aim for external behavioral conformity and end up missing the heart. *The Gospel-Centered Parent* provides a much-needed antidote to this short-sighted approach. It provides thought-provoking, practical, biblically faithful instruction for parents who yearn to model a lifestyle of faith and repentance before their children. It has proved immediately beneficial in my own parenting."

Michael R. Emlet, MDiv, MD, Faculty member and counselor at CCEF; author of *CrossTalk: Where Life and Scripture Meet.*

"Having stumbled along through the joy and the mess of parenting for almost eighteen years, it has become clear to us that one thing is needed for this magnificent calling: deep roots in the gospel. We need a grace that gives us permission to fail, and to own where we have failed with our own children. Sometimes the parent who says to a child, 'I'm sorry, will you forgive me?' is parenting better and more beautifully than the parent who makes few if any mistakes. But we also need a grace that calls us to something more, to press in with our kids with a generosity, love, and vision that calls them to be and become the very best version of their unique selves. *The Gospel-Centered Parent* is an excellent resource for this endeavor."

Scott Sauls, Senior Pastor of Christ Presbyterian Church, Nashville, TN; author of *Jesus Outside the Lines: A Way Forward for Those Who Are Tired of Taking Sides*

"It was our privilege to live in community with Jack and Rose Marie as the Lord was teaching us all about being immersed in the gospel and letting go of the illusion of being 'perfect parents.' We had a front-row seat as Jack and Rose Marie modeled the humility of parents who were becoming transparent, sharing their weaknesses and inadequacies while being bold in prayer and faith that Jesus was ALL that they needed. We shared a rocky but beautiful journey and saw God's strength in their weakness. We are indebted to them, and trust that as you go through this study you will be able to let go of your desire to control your children and grow in your desire to run to your Father for forgiveness and grace."

Dick and Liz Kaufmann, Founding Pastor of New Life Presbyterian Church, Escondido, and Harbor, a church planning network in San Diego, CA; former Executive Pastor of Redeemer Presbyterian Church NYC

THE GOSPEL-CENTERED PARENT

Rose Marie Miller, Deborah Harrell
and Jack Klumpenhower

Study Guide with Leader's Notes

New
Growth
Press

www.newgrowthpress.com

New Growth Press, Greensboro, NC 27404
Copyright © 2015 by Rose Marie Miller, Deborah Harrell, and Jack
Klumpenhower

Unless otherwise indicated, all Scripture quotations are taken from
the Holy Bible, English Standard Version®. Copyright © 2000; 2001
by Crossway Bibles, a division of Good News Publishers. Used by
permission. All rights reserved.

Scripture quotations marked (NIV) are taken from THE HOLY
BIBLE, NEW INTERNATIONAL VERSION®, NIV® Copyright ©
1973, 1978, 1984, 2011 by Biblica, Inc.® Used by permission. All rights
reserved worldwide.

Cover Design: Faceout Books, faceoutstudio.com
Typesetting: Lisa Parnell, lparnell.com

ISBN: 978-1-942572-14-5 (Print)
ISBN: 978-1-942572-15-2 (eBook)

Printed in the United States of America

22 21 20 19 18 17 16 15   1 2 3 4 5

CONTENTS

ABOUT THIS STUDY

The Gospel-Centered Parent is different from many other studies for parents. Instead of focusing on how to perform better as a parent, this study is about being a parent who lives and acts out of faith in God. Faith makes a huge difference in how we raise our children. Living by faith is not about technique. It's about trusting in Jesus, not in ourselves, and depending on him for help, hope, direction, and wisdom as we parent. As we trust in Jesus, not in our parenting techniques, we are able to rest from the pressure and anxiety we naturally feel as we raise our children.

Because it helps to practice faith with others who are learning it too, *The Gospel-Centered Parent* is meant to be studied in a group. That way, you'll learn from the insights and experiences of others and receive encouragement. The group is a place for discussion and open sharing about not only successes, but also sins and weaknesses. We, the authors of this study, will also share our own family problems and a few stories of others (with details occasionally changed to protect their identities).

Expect the usual struggles that come with a group. Some people will be cheery; some will be weary; some will be confused; and some will be sad. Some will share and others may not feel comfortable sharing. But because you'll be studying the Bible and praying together, also expect God's Spirit to work and to change people—starting with you! That's right, *The Gospel-Centered Parent* is not just about change in your children; it's mostly about gospel growth in you, the parent.

Each lesson takes a little more than an hour to complete in a group and will include these elements:

Bible Conversation. You'll start by talking about a short passage or a few verses from the Bible. It will get the group thinking and learning about the lesson's topic.

Article. The article will present the lesson's main teaching. Most articles include both Bible teaching and personal stories or reflections from one of this study's authors. We ask you to read the article aloud as a group so that you all hear the same material that you can then discuss together.

Discussion. You'll share your thoughts on the article and how it applies to your own parenting.

Exercise. The exercise is like an extended discussion question. It will help you take what you've learned and consider how it matters in your family.

Wrap-Up and Prayer. Every lesson ends with prayer. Prayer is one of the chief ways to practice faith. Rather than finish by resolving on your own to be a better mom or dad, you'll end by asking *your* loving Father to help your family and your parenting. As a parent, you have no greater resource than prayer.

In the back of the study is the **Conclusion**, a resource for you to use as you discover and apply the gospel to your parenting (adapted by Jack Klumpenhower from his book *Show Them Jesus*, New Growth Press, 2014). The **Leader's Notes** at the end of the book give direction to the group's leader(s) and sample answers for the discussion questions. Everyone can read the answers of course, but you will find it most helpful to grapple with the questions on your own before turning to the back of the book.

Obviously, *The Gospel-Centered Parent* is about the gospel—the good news of Jesus Christ. You don't have to be a believer in Jesus to join the group and start learning, but it will help if you have a basic understanding of the gospel. Even if you think you already have a good sense of what it means to be "gospel-centered," you'll likely find it helpful to read through the following parent-oriented gospel overview.

GOSPEL OVERVIEW

CREATION: GOD AND HUMANITY

The gospel is a wonderfully true story. The Bible tells us that this story began with God—the one Lord of all who exists as three persons: Father, Son, and Holy Spirit. God is infinitely powerful, glorious, good, and loving. He created the universe and everything in it to show and to share that glory.

God especially created men and women "in his own image" (Genesis 1:27). We were made to love as he loves, to practice holiness, wisdom, and truthfulness, and to help care for the rest of his world while we trust, worship, and enjoy our Creator. This gives us meaning and honor.

SIN: REBELLION AND DECAY

But humanity rejected God and his goodness. It all started with the first family, Adam and Eve, who decided they knew better than God how to run their own lives. When they refused to love, obey, and trust God, their relationship with God and others was broken. The world was plunged into rebellion and decay. The Bible calls this *sin*, and all of us are sinners (Romans 3:23). Even if we think we're pretty good compared to some people, we're still naturally inclined to put ourselves first rather than loving God and others. Even if you don't notice this so much in yourself, we can all see it on display in our children. We've lost our good purpose in God's world, to our shame.

Sin is now part of *who we are*, not just what we do. Having turned from God, selfishness and lack of love are engrained in our hearts. We are also unsatisfied, trying to find meaning and honor in poor substitutes that only pull us further from the true Lover of our souls. We end up putting our reputations, comforts, accomplishments, or even our children at the center of our lives. The Bible calls this idol worship, and the sad result is not happiness or fulfillment. Instead we end up enslaved to the very things we thought would make us happy and fulfilled.

Sin also means we are guilty before God. God made us and our world with a hard and fast rule: sin brings death. Romans 6:23 tells us, "The wages of sin is death." We are all sinners (we don't love God and people with our whole hearts, souls, and minds), so we all deserve death and separation from God forever. However, the second half of that verse turns everything around. It says, "But the free gift of God is eternal life in Christ Jesus our Lord." This is where the good news—the gospel— kicks in.

JESUS: LOVING REDEMPTION

From the time of the very first sin on earth, God showed grace. He promised that he would not abandon those who put their faith in him, but would send a Savior to defeat sin and rescue them from death. That Savior is Jesus, God the Son, who is also called Christ (meaning God's anointed, appointed one).

In love the Father sent the Son to be born as a human—one of us! So Jesus is both God and fully a man, but with one amazing difference: he has never sinned. His whole life, he loved God and people perfectly, making him the only person in the history of the world who never disobeyed God and did not deserve punishment and death.

There are many great things Jesus did, but the chief one is this: Jesus took the punishment for sin that we deserve, in our place, and instead gives us credit for all his righteousness. Because he didn't have to die for his own sins (he had none!), he was able to suffer and die on the cross as our substitute. And as the holy and eternal God, he was a sacrifice of infinite value, able to save completely everyone who has faith in him (Hebrews 7:25). Nothing demonstrates God's glory and love more than this.

VICTORY: THE WORLD RESTORED

Jesus's resurrection proves that God accepts Jesus's sacrifice for his people and has given him victory over sin, death, and every evil. Jesus has returned to heaven to reign with the Father, and now his kingdom is expanding. We, his saved people, are freed to join in the work! We spread the good news about Jesus and show his compassion every-where—beginning now, in his name and with his help, to bring healing to the world.

One day Jesus will come again to make all things new (Revelation 21:5). He will judge sin and cast out evil. He will end oppression. He will stop decay and death. The gospel isn't just about us being saved for our own sake; it's about Jesus bringing his whole creation back to glory. He will put right all that is wrong in the world and he will raise his people from the dead and bring us into glory with him, completing our rescue from sin and restoring us to God and each other in perfect relationships.

FAITH: DEPENDING ON JESUS

How do we become one of Jesus's people and share in all of this? It happens *by faith*. We accept the truth that Jesus is the Son of God our Savior, so we turn away from all our worthless and selfish pursuits (the Bible calls this *repentance*) and we pursue him instead. We also stop trusting ourselves and start trusting Jesus (the Bible calls this *faith*). For religious-minded people who may be trying to earn God's approval by being good, this means giving up any thought of being good enough to earn a place with Jesus.

That's right. Contrary to what many people think, being good doesn't save anyone from sin and death. We're saved by faith in Jesus—the only perfectly good person there is.

It's the Holy Spirit who opens our sin-wrecked hearts to believe this gospel and gives us faith, so everything about being saved is from God, not from us (Ephesians 2:8–9). The blessings God gives when we're joined to Jesus by faith are astounding. They radically change how we live, including our parenting. Consider four of the major blessings:

1. We are declared "not guilty" and perfectly right. Although we deserve punishment for sin, Jesus has already taken all that punishment. "He himself bore our sins in his body on the tree" (1 Peter 2:24). Our condemnation and shame has fallen on him, too. In its place, we get credit for his righteous living. This is "the righteousness of God through faith in Jesus Christ for all who believe" (Romans 3:22). So in the eyes of God the Judge we are both innocent and righteous forever, because we belong to the Innocent One.

Since we are declared not guilty, gospel-centered parenting means . . .

- We let go of the pressure of trying to prove ourselves through good parenting and right kids. We're free simply to love our children because our worth comes from Jesus, not them.
- We are humble, openly admitting our sins, deeply aware that we too are big sinners (just like our children) and are righteous only because of Jesus.

2. We are made children of God. "So you are no longer a slave, but a son, and if a son, then an heir through God" (Galatians 4:7). Our adoption by God gives us all the privileges any child has. Our Father loves us. He takes care of us. He listens to our prayers. He trains and disciplines us. He shares everything he has with us, and intends for us to be his forever.

Because we are God's children, gospel-centered parenting means . . .

- We aren't consumed with building our family's reputation or image, but instead find joy in being part of God's family.
- We are dependent and child-like parents, praying often as we trust our own heavenly Father for every family need.

3. We become loving people. God doesn't just leave us miserable and sinful; he begins transforming us. The Holy Spirit empowers and trains us to love God and others from the heart—to be like Jesus. In this life we taste only the beginnings of this triumph over self-centeredness and sinful desires, and at times our progress may seem frustratingly slow, but the fight is on! We are being changed "from one degree of glory to another" (2 Corinthians 3:18).

Because we are growing to be like Jesus, gospel-centered parenting means . . .

- We are confident and patient with our children, even when they persist in disobeying. We keep teaching them God's ways and humbly showing them his love.
- We use the Spirit's tools with our children—prayer, the Word of God, and the gospel message—rather than our own wisdom or nagging.

4. We are given eternal life. Jesus's resurrection means we have new life too. Even though our lives in this world include suffering and death, we have the promise of resurrection and a future inheritance kept in heaven for us. We will have a share in Christ's restoration of all things. Best of all, "we will always be with the Lord" (1 Thessalonians 4:17).

Since we have eternal life, gospel-centered parenting means . . .

- We don't live for our children's success or worldly happiness, and we teach them not to live for it either. Our hope is in Jesus.
- We are not undone by suffering or family disappointments. We know these will not last.

This is the gospel story. It's all about Jesus but, as you can see, we become part of it through our faith in him. Faith and repentance are ongoing; the constant core of a gospel-centered parent's life. This can be challenging but it is also thrilling. It's a way of life that changes everything—because Jesus changes everything.

lesson

1

TRUSTING GOD TO BUILD YOUR FAMILY

BIG IDEA

The core of a gospel-centered parent is *faith in God*. All we do flows from this. It's all too easy to view our parenting as work we must properly carry out and to see our children's character, abilities, appearance, success in school, faithfulness to Jesus—and so much else—as verdicts on our performance. But the truth is that God builds the house. Nothing we do as parents is more important than that we be humbled; that we turn our trust away from ourselves and to our Lord who blesses his families. Then with God's help we become able to resist worry, fear, anger, control, blame—and every other parent-sin that keeps us up at night.

BIBLE CONVERSATION *15 minutes*

In Psalm 127, Solomon writes about safety and prosperity for a household and its community. The psalm deals with a question we often ask ourselves: *will my family be all right?* **Read all of Psalm 127.** (Have someone in the group read the psalm aloud.)

(1) Even in tasks like bricklaying and keeping watch, where the skill and diligence of the worker would seem critical, what is the true source of a family's success?

(2) Long ago, a theologian summarized Psalm 127 by writing, "The order of the home and its success are maintained solely by the blessing of God—not by the policy, diligence and wisdom of men."[1] What besides God are you most tempted to trust for your family's success? Is it your *policies*, your *diligence*, or your *wisdom*? Share an example.

Example: Say what you mean, Mean what you say

(3) Starting from the descriptions in verse 2, how might the temperament of a parent who trusts God differ from a must-do-it-myself parent?

(4) Having many children might seem only to multiply a parent's frustrations. Why do you think Solomon can instead call many children a blessing? How might the frustrations that come with even one child be more manageable when we trust that "the LORD builds the house"?

****

We seldom find it easy or "natural" to be parents who trust God to build the house. In the following article, Rose Marie tells how God increased her parenting faith, and what a difference it made in her family. (Take turns reading the article aloud, switching readers at the paragraph breaks.)

---

[1] John Calvin, *Commentary on Psalms*, trans. James Anderson. http://www.ccel .org/ccel/calvin/calcom12.xi.html.

lesson

ARTICLE

UNLESS THE LORD BUILDS THE HOUSE

10 minutes

Even though it was many years ago, I clearly remember the first time I really heard Psalm 127. We had just moved from California for my husband to go to seminary, and I was sitting in the back row of a church in Philadelphia. Our three young children were with me as I tried to listen to the sermon (that's how we did it back in the day!), and I was trying to keep them quiet with snacks, books, and crayons. Usually I had a hard time concentrating, but that Sunday I heard every word.

The pastor read to us, "Unless the LORD builds the house, those who build it labor in vain" (Psalm 127:1). He said that one way God is building his kingdom is through families that love Jesus, and parents are called by God to participate with him in this great work. As I sat there with my children climbing all over me, I felt as if I had received a personal commission from God. My family was to be part of God's kingdom! Despite all of the weariness that came with caring for little ones, I felt that I had a clear purpose in life.

Soon we had not just three children, but five, and we did work hard at building them into godly, respectful Christians. We taught them Bible stories, memorized Scripture and catechism questions, sang hymns (completely off key!), and sent them to Christian schools. But somehow, in the midst of all of these good things, we lost sight of who was doing the building. Instead of participating with God in his work, it

10

became all our work. We also left out the gospel—the good news that Jesus came to die for sinners.

How could that be when from Genesis to Revelation we read about the good news of God's faithfulness to rescue his people from sin and death and change sinners into eternal worshipers? Yet, somehow in the busyness of training our children to learn good manners, behave in public, do well in school, and be obedient to us, we forgot the grand message that we are all broken by sin and need to go to Jesus, our Savior, for forgiveness and help every day. We forgot to live by faith in front of our children.

What is faith? Simply put, it's trusting in the work of another. Psalm 127 tells us to trust the work of God to build our family. We believed that, but we didn't go far enough. We didn't see that trusting in the work of God had to be applied to our life together as broken sinners. We didn't share with our children that we need to daily turn to Christ by faith for forgiveness and that they could do the same. We forgot to share the good news that you don't have to save yourself or defeat death. All of that is provided by the work of Jesus on the cross for us. Our part is receiving it by faith.

Psalm 127 tells us what happens when we don't live by faith. We eat "the bread of anxious toil" (v. 2) and all we do turns out to be "in vain." We all respond differently when children struggle, but the general themes are the same—we become anxious, afraid, angry, controlling, and/or give up in despair. Often those struggles are accompanied by over-whelming fear.

If we think it is all up to us, then we do have much to fear. I talk with parents from all over the world who share their fears with me. How will their children turn out? Who will keep them safe? Will they make a bad choice that destroys their life? I understand why they are afraid. We look at our inadequacies as parents, the influence of the culture, and our children's struggles and somehow we think we have to come up with a plan to save them.

This was certainly true in our family. We worked hard to get our children to obey outwardly, but we never thought to talk about what was going on in their hearts. Unintentionally we taught them a works-oriented religion. This wasn't our theology (we certainly knew better), but it was our daily practice. And for a while it seemed like it was working. Our children were well behaved, knew the Bible, and could craft a great public prayer.

But hearts that are not changed are eventually revealed. The first inkling I had that all of our efforts to build our family into God's house were not going as I planned was when our eighteen-year-old daughter Barbara angrily left home and faith.[2] I was filled with fear and questions about how God could have let this happen. I didn't realize it at the time, but Barbara and I were very much alike (although I was much better behaved!). Her lack of faith exposed my own lack of faith. I felt the weight of failure. All my hard work had turned out to be "in vain," and I blamed God and others for the unexpectedly poor result of all of my work in my daughter's life.

But despite my anger and fear, God was still at work. Right at the point where I felt my failure most keenly, God did his work, his way. Of course he started not with our daughter, but with my husband and me. His work in us began with a total teardown! We had to see that our plans, abilities, gifts, education, and desires were not the building blocks of faith. Pride, arrogance, and presumption lay deeply rooted in my heart, and were only dealt with by going to the cross. I knew the facts of the gospel, but not the person at the center. Jesus builds his kingdom with the poor and needy; not with good people or good children, but with those who know they need a Savior.

In our weakness, as we learned that our only hope for ourselves and our children was the work of Jesus, God did his work of building faith in us. Psalm 127 ends with a promise that our children are a gift from God and that he will use them in his kingdom (vv. 3–5). Many years

---

[2] For the full story, see *Come Back, Barbara* (P&R, 1997), the book that Rose Marie's husband, C. John Miller, and their daughter Barbara Miller Juliani coauthored.

ago I had glimpsed that truth, but I had to learn that my part in it was moment-by-moment faith. That's how I learned to trust Jesus, the builder of everything (Hebrews 3:3–4), to build my family into his kingdom. His work is still going on—in me, in my children, my grand-children, and my great-grandchildren. God is using all of us. But not out of *our* strength, only out of our reliance on *his* strength. My prayer for you, as you go through this study, is that you will learn to put all of your trust in Jesus, the builder of everything, and will learn to rely on him daily as you go about the hard work of caring for your children and sharing with them the good news that Jesus has paid it all.

DISCUSSION *15 minutes*

(5) What parts of Rose Marie's early parenting sound familiar when you think of your own family?

(6) How might your parenting be different if you trusted more in God to build your house? What might you *do* (or stop doing) to practice faith in him?

(7) Why is it so important for parents to deeply believe (not just know as a point of doctrine) that they are completely forgiven in Jesus?

AM I A GOSPEL-CENTERED PARENT?

20 minutes

Let's think about the difference between parents who are focused first on themselves or their children and parents who are gospel-centered. Gospel-centered parents focus first on God. They know that they too are children. They have a heavenly Father who loves them and builds their families.

The following chart shows several ways this difference might play out in our lives as parents. Read the descriptions and pick one or two areas where you particularly want to grow to be a more gospel-centered parent. Share these with the group. (If an item doesn't fit you perfectly, share the part that *does* fit.) Try to give an example from your parenting of your need to grow in that area.

Self/Child-Centered Parents	Gospel-Centered Parents
Live with anxiety over their children's faith, safety, education, future, or other concerns.	**Live with faith** that God controls the future. Strive more to be faithful to him while worrying less about where that might lead.
Feel pressure to do parenting correctly and win approval from their spouse, family, other parents, or God. Often compare their family to other families.	**Know they already enjoy the favor of God** through Jesus who died for them, so are free to parent in love, not out of pressure to impress.
May get angry when children fail to meet behavior or achievement expectations. Blame their children, spouse, or others.	**Are humble**, knowing how much they too need God's help and forgiveness—making them able to teach, encourage, and warn their children patiently.
Seldom pray, preferring to focus on fixing problems by themselves.	**Pray constantly** about both big and little family concerns, trusting their Father to help.
Seldom admit their sins, preferring to be a voice of authority and virtue to their children.	**Often admit their sins** and their need for a Savior, allowing them to effectively point their children to Jesus as well.
Are controlling toward their children, either overbearing or manipulative, feeling a need to make sure everything goes right.	**Trust that God is in control** and is the wiser Father. Are chiefly concerned with guiding their children toward him.
May withdraw from their children, especially when problems or spiritual matters arise, out of fear they'll fail or be exposed as flawed parents.	Are confident that their Father will use even their flaws and failures for good, so prayerfully **engage even the most difficult family problems.**
May be resentful toward God or others when things don't go as they want or when their children disappoint them.	**Learn surrender, comfort, and forgiveness** from their Father who has forgiven them.

Self/Child-Centered Parents	Gospel-Centered Parents
Set aside all else to pursue academic, athletic, or other dreams for their children—and may be **devastated by setbacks.**	**Believe and teach their children that God loves them** and works all things for their good, even amid disappointments and suffering.
Feel content only when their children are happy, achieving, and faithful.	**Find satisfaction in God alone**, letting them care for their children rather than worship family success.
Add your own self/child-centered behavior:	Add your own gospel-centered behavior:

WRAP-UP AND PRAYER *10 minutes*

Sometimes an exercise like the one we just completed only makes us feel guilty. Resist this by remembering that *the Lord builds the house.* Your Father knows you are weak and sinful. He loves you anyway, and gives his Spirit to help you. *He* is the one who grants blessings to your family—and faith to you! The descriptions of a gospel-centered parent can encourage you even if you don't yet live up to them very well, because with God's help they are possible.

The coming lessons will explore many of these themes further. For right now, let's begin to practice faith-filled parenting by praying together for our families. Include prayers that God would make you into a gospel-centered parent.

2

THE PARENT AS
THE CHIEF REPENTER

BIG IDEA

Repentance is being sorry for sin and turning away from it, so that by faith you move toward God and life with him. It is an inner brokenness and change worked by the Holy Spirit and lived out daily by us. All parents can tell you exactly how their children need to repent, but often we don't pay enough attention to our need for ongoing repentance. And even when we do struggle against sin, we tend to hide our deepest struggles from our children lest they see what big sinners we really are. Sadly, this deprives them of what they most need from us in order to repent for themselves—our example.

BIBLE CONVERSATION *15 minutes*

Let's learn about repentance from Psalm 51. The psalm is King David's prayer after he was caught in some particularly evil sins; committing adultery with the wife of one of his most loyal soldiers and arranging the man's death to cover it up.

(1) **Read verses 1–6.** David's repentance includes acknowledging the full ugliness of his sin. How is it more than just a one-time mistake? How is the sin more than an outward act? How is the sin more than just hurting his fellow man?

(2) **Read verses 7–12.** Would you say David's repentance is about trying hard to do better or about turning to God and trusting his mercy? Besides forgiveness, what more does David ask from God?

(3) **Read verses 13–17.** How will David's repentance in turn help others to repent? What will they notice about David when they see his repentance?

****

Like David tried to mask his adultery, it's common for us initially to hide, excuse, or justify our sin. To repent, we need more than a change in outward behavior or mere sorrow over sin. We need a brokenness produced by the Holy Spirit that gives up on hiding and excuse-making. Then we can rest in our Father's love instead of in our self-made reputations, and become open and honest with others—even our children. If our kids are going to learn by example how to live humbly before God, they will constantly need to be around humble people (us!) who repent openly.

In this article, Rose Marie tells how God showed both her and her husband how vital it was to repent daily and confess their weakness in front of their children. (Take turns reading the article aloud, switching readers at the paragraph breaks.)

lesson

ARTICLE

2

LIVING THE GOSPEL IN FRONT OF YOUR FAMILY

10 minutes

In a sixth-grade Sunday school class our daughter Barbara attended, the teacher said, "You kids think that Christianity is just a list of dos and don'ts." Later Barbara told us that story and said she thought, "Well if it's not about being good, then what is it about?" Sadly, she had no idea that forgiveness for sins, not right behavior, was the heart of the gospel message, and apparently none of the Christian adults in her life (including us), helped her understand that either.

After his resurrection, Jesus proclaimed that "repentance and forgiveness of sins" was the message that his disciples would bring to all nations (Luke 24:47), but often it is not the message that Christian parents share with their children. Most of us know that God calls us to train up our children in the way they should go (Proverbs 22:6). We usually take this verse to mean that we should teach our children the Bible, good morals, and the right way to behave. And it does! But it means so much more.

The "way" is the good news of forgiveness for sins that Jesus purchased for us on the cross. The "way" is a whole new life of daily faith and repentance. If we want our children to go this way, it has to start with us not only sharing the gospel with them, but also living it before them. We make it easy for our children to miss the gospel and think that the Bible is just a set of rules, if that's all we share with them.

I grew up in a German household where good manners, respect for authority, and going to church on Sundays were the code by which we lived. My husband, Jack, came from a pioneer family in Oregon that had many of the same values. Even though we became Christians, what we lived and modeled for our children was the idea that if you worked hard and treated people well God would bless you. That was the gospel according to the Millers! But that is not the gospel of Jesus Christ. Although these are all good qualities to instill in your children, because we made them our primary focus there was no room for relying on God, for God to search the heart, and for repentance on deeper levels.

We didn't share with our children our own daily need of a Savior. So they had no idea that they needed Jesus every day as well. Later Jack said, "If I could go back again, I would have done so much more to open up and show my children how Christ helped me with my weaknesses."[3] But sadly, at that time, Jack and I thought that being a Christian meant hiding your weaknesses and sins from others—including our own children. The result? Our daughter Barbara thought that Christianity couldn't be for her because she wasn't a good person and you had to be good to be a Christian.

We had forgotten that we all stumble in many ways (James 3:2). Not just children, but parents as well need to daily ask God "to create in me a pure heart" (Psalm 51:10). Jack was the first to see himself as a great sinner who needed to repent daily and ask for daily help and forgiveness. As he did that, he was able to go to Barbara and ask her why she was so angry with him. She told him that it was because he acted like he was never wrong. He asked her for forgiveness. That might have been the first time one of us told a child we were sorry! It was probably the first honest conversation they had.

I was a bit slower, but God used Barbara's rebellion to expose my pride, reliance on rules instead of God, and judgment of others. It was a painful time, but when the Spirit brought deep conviction of my pride,

---

[3] C. John Miller, *Saving Grace: Daily Devotions from Jack Miller* (Greensboro: New Growth Press, 2014), October 26 entry.

arrogance, and presumption, I knew that "Against you and you only have I sinned" (Psalm 51:4). The conviction and the cleansing was so powerful that it sent me home to forgive my own mother who had brought destruction to our home, and to ask my children to forgive me for all the legalism (the lifestyle of rule-keeping without reference to Christ) that I had taught them.

Jack and I brought the gospel to our parenting late. You can't share the gospel with your children if you aren't living it, and it took the work of the Spirit in our lives to show us that we were sinners who needed to turn to Jesus, not just once for eternal cleansing, but every day as in him we enjoy God's fatherly forgiveness anew. But the amazing thing was how the Spirit used our feeble, too-late sharing of the good news that Christ died for sinners. The Spirit used us, in our weaknesses, to live the gospel in front of our children. As Barbara said later, "Hearing you share your sins and ask for forgiveness didn't change me—God did. But it did catch my attention."

David says in Psalm 51, "Surely I was sinful at birth, sinful from the time my mother conceived me" (v. 5). This is true of all of us—parents and children alike. How can sinners live with sinners? It starts by acknowledging that not just children need to "say sorry" but parents as well. Because we know we are forgiven, we don't have to hide our sins; instead we can ask our children for forgiveness when we sin against them. And, when they see our sins on display (as surely they will more than anyone else), we can acknowledge that we need Jesus just as much as they do. We can lead our children to Jesus and teach them the true gospel by being the chief repenters in our homes.

As parents, we instinctively know that the job of keeping our children safe and helping them grow into people who love God and others is far beyond us. We know that God has to do this work. He has to be with us and help us. He is the builder of everything—our children included. But it is easy to forget that to invite him into our hearts and homes, every day we need to humbly go to him for forgiveness and help. God dwells in a high and holy place but also with him who has a humble and contrite heart (Isaiah 57:15).

DISCUSSION *15 minutes*

(4) How was Rose Marie's initial idea of what it means to live as a Christian like or unlike your own ideas?

(5) Think about the impact it had on Rose Marie to see her husband admit his weakness and sin to their daughter. She began doing the same with even more people in her life! Have you experienced anything similar from being around particularly humble or open believers? Tell about it.

(6) Consider how often you talk to your children about *their* sins compared to how often you talk about your own. How might your relationship with your children change if you admitted your weakness and sin to them more often?

WHAT'S YOUR FAMILY CODE?

20 minutes

Rose Marie wrote about how the "Miller way" made good manners, respect for authority, and Sunday churchgoing her *family's code*. Think about what your own family code might be. What besides repentance and faith in Jesus have you instilled as chief behavior goals for your children? Once you've come up with your answers, discuss your findings with the group.

1. Examine the clues. To hone in on what your family code might be, start by completing the following sentences:

The chief behavior rules (whether they were religious rules or non-religious ones) of the family I grew up in were _____

_____ .

If I were to ask my children, "What do I *most* want from you behavior-wise?" they might say I want them to _____

_____ .

It drives me crazy when my kids _____

_____ .

2. Identify your family code. Now use those clues to think about what behaviors you try to create in your children *that seem to them more important than confession of sin and faith in Jesus.* This is your family code. It's what your children feel they must do if you are to consider them good people. It may consist of excellent principles that are commanded by God, but it still competes with the core of what it means to be a Christian.

The family code I'm instilling in my children is_____

_____ .

3. See how to repent. Jesus is not for good people. He's for people who admit their sin, receive forgiveness in him, and repent. Think about some ways your interactions with your children would change if this principle consistently mattered more to you than your family code.

My interactions with my children would involve less _____

_____ .

My interactions with my children would include more_____

_____ .

4. Begin repenting of your family code. Parents who find joy in being forgiven in Jesus become (1) humble enough to ask questions, (2) willing to admit sin, and (3) eager to share what Jesus has done for them. So when you're back with your children, consider doing this:

- **Ask questions.** Ask them what behavior they think you most want from them, or any of the other questions from step one. Or ask them, "If there's one thing you would change about me or the way we interact, what would that be?"
- **Confess.** Start your confession by confessing the code itself. Admit to your children how you've stressed the wrong things, and ask their forgiveness (yes, you can do this without diminishing your parental authority).

- **Tell.** Share with them about how Jesus forgives both you and them, and the joy this gives you despite your sin.

WRAP-UP AND PRAYER *10 minutes*

True repentance requires a heart that comes to hate sin and delights in Jesus. This is not worked up by willpower, but rather *received* from the Holy Spirit. So start by praying that God will give you grace to be humble, admit your sin, and truly repent. Pray together now.

3

TEACHING YOUR CHILD "ON THE WAY"

BIG IDEA

As parents we have a duty to teach our children to trust and obey Jesus. We also *want* them to come to faith and make godly choices. These twin pressures of duty and desire often make us seek a sure-proof formula for pounding the gospel into our children—but there is no such thing. Rather than a few easy steps, it's a long walk. Our job is to make Jesus such a constant part of everyday family life that our kids both hear about him and learn by our example *all the time*. This is a huge challenge. But because it's all about Jesus rather than about our performance, it's also joyous and freeing with all of the resources of the Spirit of Christ available as we ask.

BIBLE CONVERSATION *15 minutes*

The book of Deuteronomy is a collection of instructions for God's people. These instructions were given after God had rescued the people from Egypt and was about to bring them into the Promised Land. Chapter 6 is one of the most famous passages in the Old Testament; a summary of what life with God in the land he is giving should look like. **Read Deuteronomy 6:4–12.** (Have someone in the group read the passage aloud.)

(1) Try to describe in a single word or phrase what this passage says devotion to God should be like. What are some words you might choose?

(2) To love God *with all your heart* is a tall order. What in this passage helps believers keep God's Word on their hearts?

(3) Let's think about our own lives. What routines or events help you to think about God as you go through a typical day?

(4) What unearned blessings has God given you that you need to be sure not to forget, so that your heart stays tuned toward him?

* * * *

You probably noticed that teaching these things to our children was included in the passage. Read the article below, in which Jack shares some thoughts about teaching our kids. (Take turns reading the article aloud, switching readers at the paragraph breaks.)

lesson

TALKING ABOUT JESUS "ON THE WAY"

10 minutes

Jesus called Deuteronomy 6:5 the greatest commandment: "You shall love the LORD your God with all your heart and with all your soul and with all your might." That's a strict, sweeping law that might make us gulp even without the verses that follow, which contain some of the strongest instructions to parents anywhere in the Bible. It turns out that in addition to obeying the Greatest Commandment, we're ordered to teach it (and all the others) to our children.

Oh, the pressure! We hear rules about what it should mean to teach our kids in the house or by the way, and perhaps we feel guilty when we fail to follow whatever formula is being offered—or maybe we don't teach them at all. Maybe we feel overwhelmed by the challenge.

Well, following these instructions does make for a wild adventure. It isn't just about teaching our children; it also requires much spiritual renewal in *us*! But this does not mean we should become model families that look like they belong in a cheesy greeting card photo. Our Father has filled his instructions with comfort, encouragement—and much freedom.

Six Freedoms (and Challenges) in Deuteronomy 6

1. RELAX. You don't have to follow someone else's formula. Teaching our kids about Jesus should happen as we sit and walk and lie down and rise—as we go about life (v. 7). God's instructions allow for a wide variety of times and methods. That means there is no formula! We have great freedom to mold our gospel teaching to fit what works for our family life, not force it to fit the way some expert says it must be done. We dare not neglect it, but we need not follow any particular model.

2. ACT. You do have to be deliberate. Despite our freedom, we must "teach them diligently" (v. 7). It takes purposeful action to get started teaching about Jesus, and to keep going. The times when we sit (mealtime), walk (travel time), lie down (bedtime), and rise (morning) actually make excellent occasions to set good habits. And our doorframes and gates might make handy places to post daily reminders of God. Especially in a family that feels awkward talking about Jesus, establishing set times to pray together, learn, and read the Bible can help overcome the awkwardness. For busy families (isn't that all families?), having a short, set time to talk about God will help you to keep this in your schedule. Planned prayer and teaching times train us to pray and think of Jesus in unplanned moments as well. Try any way you can think of to look to Jesus as a family several times a day, so that he fills your lives always.

3. SMILE. It's not all about enforcing rules. Yes, our kids must learn to obey God. But the obedience in Deuteronomy 6 flows from gratitude, confidence, and hope in him. Even when children ask about God's law, the text instructs parents to tell of salvation. "Then you shall say to your son, 'We were Pharaoh's slaves in Egypt. And the LORD brought us out of Egypt with a mighty hand'" (v. 21). This salvation includes:

- What God has *already* done (vv. 12, 21–23)
- How he cares *now* and provides life-giving laws (vv. 1–3, 24–25)
- How he will bless *in the future* (vv. 10–11)

For us, this means we must teach our children all about salvation in Jesus. What a joy it is to tell about the forgiveness that's already ours because he died for our sins and rose again, or the fatherly care we have today because he shares his Father with us, or the future hope of being with him forever! We get to share that whole gospel story, not just lay down rules. More than that, we also get to wonder at Jesus himself. We can be amazed at how he kept the law for our sake, not just worry over how we break it. The love of God will grow in children when they know Jesus and fall in love with him—because they've heard the gospel and believe. We find it easy to correct our children all the time, as life happens. Let's tell them about Jesus all the time too.

4. GO DEEP. Make it about your heart. We will find it impossible to keep on telling our children about Jesus if our hearts aren't in it, and difficult to stop if they are. This is why we're told, "These words that I command you today shall be on your heart" (v. 6). Being committed to a personal practice of prayer, Bible reading, and churchgoing may sound tiresome, but it's actually how we pour God's good news into our own hearts first. This is more than fuel; it's how we learn joy in our Savior. It makes the task of doing these same things with our children delightful.

5. BE REAL. You need integrity. Since Jesus is not just for special activities, there's no pretending. We must be the same person at home or while travelling as we are at church. If we teach about Jesus while we go about everyday life, without gearing up to look extra spiritual, our children surely won't think we're mega-gifted (or sinless) teachers. They'll see who we really are—and we need to let them see! They must know that following Jesus is not for "good people," but for those who are weak, make mistakes, and need grace for each moment. This kind of integrity is wondrously freeing, but can also be scary. Many parents fear letting their kids see their failures, or even their ordinariness. Yet we must not ignore the fact that this great parenting passage of the Bible says absolutely nothing about how capable we must be, and much about how real we must be.

6. TRUST. Keep your eyes on Jesus. We'll be teaching our children that there is no lasting source of happiness except for Jesus. They must trust no other helper, serve no other master, and seek only the true Lover of their souls. Teaching this is as glorious and necessary as any task on earth, so it means we too will be forced to turn constantly to Jesus. That's the only way to accept the Deuteronomy 6 challenge without collapsing under the pressure. When we fail (and we will fail so often!), we must rest in the fact that Jesus never fails. When we sin, we must remember that he forgives and still loves us (1 John 1:9–10).

Does any of this sound too hard? Remember our first lesson: the Lord builds the house. Do not forget to go to your Father in prayer. He strengthens weak people and also uses their continuing weakness to accomplish great things. It's okay to be weak, because then you are strong (2 Corinthians 12:10).

DISCUSSION *15 minutes*

(5) Was anything in the article different from the way you've noticed that Christians typically think about teaching their children to be godly? How does the article point you in a different direction than the way you tend to teach your kids?

(6) Which of the six points sounds most challenging to you, and why? Which sounds most freeing?

lesson

EXERCISE

START SMALL, DREAM BIG

20 minutes

Now dream about how you might be able to apply these principles as you train your children. Think about starting to do one thing you don't do now. (Relax, you aren't committing to do it, just beginning to think and dream.) We'll do this build-a-dream style; picking elements one at a time in three steps. After you've built your full child-teaching idea, share it with the group. *NOTE: Encourage sharing in the group by agreeing not to hold another person's feet to the fire about doing these things immediately—especially if the other person is your spouse! No one will want to bring up ideas if they think they're going to be hounded about them later. Use this exercise only to stir up desires, which ultimately will lead to taking action in some way.*

Step 1: Pick an opportunity. This is a time or place that fits your family's lifestyle and is an opportunity to be with your children. It might be:

- A time of day
- A particular meal
- Some daily travel
- A frequent piece of work or chores
- Some other opportunity that might work for you

Step 2: Add an activity. This is something from the lesson that you would like to do more often. It might have to do with:

- Praying with your children
- Bible/story reading
- Bible study and discussion
- Talking/reading/learning about Jesus
- Encouraging with the gospel and the blessings included in salvation
- Worshiping as a family
- Sharing your own sin/struggles and your repentance/progress in Christ
- A way to care for others in Jesus's name
- Your personal spiritual life
- Some other teaching-type activity that you would like to do

Step 3: Add some encouragement for yourself. This is something that will help keep your dream a joyful challenge rather than a burdensome one, even if you end up not being very good at the task. It might be:

- Remembering how completely you're forgiven in Jesus
- Remembering how God loves to use you even in your failures and weaknesses—often *especially* in those things
- A Bible passage or prayer that keeps you focused on Jesus
- Something else from this lesson that you found encouraging

WRAP-UP AND PRAYER *10 minutes*

Perhaps, after all this, bringing gospel truth into your family life still seems an impossible task. It is, of course, without God. Trying to do these things by sheer willpower won't work—it just won't! Instead, we need to start by asking our heavenly Father to help us. He doesn't ask his children to go forward without his help. Jesus said, "I will not leave you as orphans; I will come to you" (John 14:18). You are not alone in this task. The very thing that God calls you to, he also promises that he will help you with. He is committed to you. He is committed to your child. He wants to teach you both about himself. Begin by praying for that now.

4

DISCIPLINE BY FAITH, NOT FRUSTRATION

BIG IDEA

Training our children to obey is a difficult task, in part because our own sins often get in the way. We know that our discipline should be done in love, the way God disciplines us, but our selfish desires for control, for respect, or for risk-free parenting get mixed in with our love. Thankfully, our heavenly Father is the perfect parent we aren't able to be. As we turn to him in faith and repentance, he helps us to rest in his love and acceptance so we are free to love our children rather than demand that they satisfy our desires. And through the gospel he can also work the change in our children that they need most: transformed hearts.

BIBLE CONVERSATION *15 minutes*

Near the end of Ephesians, the book is about relationships within the home in light of our submission to God. Read the part about children and parents from **Ephesians 6:1–4**. (Have someone read the passage aloud.)

(1) What do you think it means for children to obey their parents "in the Lord"?

(2) What are some things that will first have to be true of our parenting if our children are to obey "in the Lord" and because of their hope in God's promises?

(3) What are the two instructions to fathers? Give an example of how a parent might do both at the same time. (Note that Paul is addressing fathers because they would have been responsible for discipline, but his directive applies to both moms and dads.)

These difficult commands are followed by an instruction to "be strong in the Lord and in the strength of his might" (v. 10). Have someone **read Ephesians 6:14–18**.

(4) The difficult task of parenting is done by taking up God's armor: truth, righteousness, the gospel, faith, salvation, the Word of God, and prayer. In a few words, summarize how that affects the way we parent our children.

****

Training our children to be obedient is about both their faith and ours. It this article, Debbie shares how she learned this. (Read the article aloud, switching readers at the paragraph breaks.)

ARTICLE

WHEN YOUR "OR ELSE" PLAN FAILS

10 minutes

I sat on our stairs with my head bowed and my heart racing. A few steps above me sat my young daughter, her face streaked with hot, angry tears. She was angry and I was furious. I was a teacher, so I knew all about creating a well-thought-out, consistent, age-appropriate discipline plan. It was my specialty. I also knew that parents are put in authority over their children (I had this part of the job description down). But my idea of authority was, "Do what I say, or else . . ." My daughter had never tested the "or else" part—until now. And sadly, I didn't actually have an "or else" plan.

I had used my authority only to make sure she obeyed outwardly, and today that plan had failed. Ephesians 6 echoed through the red haze that wanted to overtake me. "Children, obey your parents in the Lord, for this is right. 'Honor your father and mother' (this is the first commandment with a promise), 'that it may go well with you and that you may live long in the land.' Fathers, do not provoke your children to anger, but bring them up in the discipline and instruction of the Lord" (vv. 1–4). I knew that it was right to require obedience from my daughter, and I had, but the last part of the verse was what I was struggling with most. To "provoke" our children means that we act in a way that tempts them to become annoyed, angry, or bitter. By letting my anger get out of control, I had done that with my daughter.

Discipline is hard because we do have to correct our children when they sin, but often our own sins muddle the process. Colossians 3:21 warns us about what happens when we provoke our children: *"they become discouraged."* Discouraged kids may feel ashamed, resentful, or powerless. They might eventually do what we want, but they won't do it with any hope in Jesus. They'll feel conquered, not trained; powerless to resist rather than empowered to obey. None of us wants this for our children, but provoking them comes naturally because we are sinners parenting sinners.

The discipline of our children is meant to be done out of love, the way God parents *us*. Hebrews 12:6 says, "The Lord disciplines the ones he loves, and chastises every son whom he receives." We want to be like that. We do want to correct our children because we love them and want the best for them, but often our selfish desires to be in control, to be respected, or to look good get mixed in with our love. And because our children are selfish too and also want to look good and be in control, our attempts to discipline often result in everyone—parents and children—becoming frustrated and angry.

At the time of the incident on the steps, my husband and I had just started taking the Serge course called *Sonship*, about living as God's dearly loved sons and daughters (Romans 8:15; Galatians 4:5–6). We were learning how we have a loving Father who already says we "look good" in his eyes, and how this helps us to be loving rather than selfish.

As I sat on the steps below my daughter, I wondered how these truths could apply to parenting. Thus far my discipline plan was to micro-manage outward behaviors so that my daughter's obedience was motivated by fear of punishment or consequences. But I realized that instead, I needed to take the gospel into my own heart, and then invite my daughter to believe it too. I had to step back, pray, and look below my daughter's surface sins to address her heart. What struggle with pride or fear made her unwilling to be corrected? She needed to know that God gives help to overcome it. She needed to hear how, despite her misbehavior, she has a loving Father who forgives her in Jesus. She needed to see how repenting would be a joyful return to her Father's love and care (Luke 15:20–24). And she needed to see that I believed those things, too, about my own sin.

Our ultimate goal is not just to get our children to submit to us, but to train their hearts to submit to God. For this, they need a heart that's broken by Christ's love. They must hear the gospel in our discipline and see the gospel lived out in how we talk with them about their sins and apply the appropriate consequences. Responding in selfish anger to our children's sins is not how our heavenly Father responds to us when we sin. And our anger does not bring about the righteous life that God desires for our children (James 1:20).

Later that night as I prayed and read bedtime stories with my daughter, she handed me a picture she had drawn to illustrate that morning. The picture showed one large dragon and one small dragon breathing fire at one another. I didn't like seeing myself portrayed as an angry, fire-breathing dragon, but it was a good illustration of how the morning had gone. It also created a good opportunity for us both to repent and pray.

Going to Jesus for forgiveness and help brings healing to parents and children. As we ask for the Spirit's help, he trains us to act out of love (because we've been loved!) rather than out of a need for respect and order. The Bible provides no direct instructions for how we should address most everyday situations that come up in parenting, especially the simple discipline that creates safe boundaries and manages routines. Daily discipline takes constant wisdom that comes from God. Such wisdom makes us both patient and firm. When we ourselves know we're secure in the undeserved love of our Father, we have both the humility to be gentle and the courage to engage even tough discipline cases where the risk of failure seems high.

DISCUSSION *10 minutes*

(5) The article says, "Discipline is hard because we do have to correct our children when they sin, but often our own sins muddle the process." Which of your sins most tend to get in the way when you discipline your children? *Pride, Stubborn-ness*

(6) Give an example of how being "secure in the undeserved love of our Father" might make you humble when you correct your child? Why might it also give you courage to engage tough cases rather than withdrawing?

Because it's about the childs learning + we can be unattatched because we are teachers of God's love

lesson

EXERCISE

GROWING IN LOVING DISCIPLINE

25 minutes

Think of a recent example of a discipline session with a disobedient child. It will help to pick a time that went less than perfectly. Evaluate it according to the chart below (check all that apply), and be ready to share your findings with the group.

Some **good, loving reasons** behind *why* I disciplined my child and *how* I went about it were:

- ☒ The child had done wrong and needed to be corrected.
- ☐ I wanted the child ultimately to learn to obey and respect God, and that includes learning to obey and respect me.
- ☐ I saw it as an opportunity to encourage the child with the gospel.
- ☐ Other: _____

_____

Some **selfish, sinful reasons** mixed in with my discipline were:

- ☒ I felt disrespected or unable to assert my authority, and I wanted to regain respect or control for my own sake.
- ☐ The child had embarrassed me and I wanted the child to feel some of that sting and shame.
- ☒ The child's behavior was interfering with other goals in my life (getting out of the house on time, getting my work done

properly, having peace and quiet, etc.) and I took the easiest path to getting my goals back on track.

☐ Other: _____

_____

Some **helpful actions** that were part of my discipline were:

☒ I stopped sinful or harmful behavior before it could grow worse.

☐ I dealt with the child's heart, addressing the idols, fears, and stubbornness underneath the child's outward sin.

☐ I took time to pray and talk about Jesus with the child.

☐ Other: _____

_____

Some **harmful actions** that were part of my discipline were:

☐ I acted out of anger over what had happened to me.

☐ I enforced more control than necessary or wouldn't let the discipline session end until I was clearly the winner.

☒ I disengaged, let the deepest problems go unresolved, failed to follow up, or otherwise gave up on discipline due to fear or exhaustion.

☐ Other: _____

_____

Having evaluated a discipline session, I most want to grow in gospel parenting by

Getting pride out of way,
take More time & tend to
deeper issues

Some things that can change in my own heart that will help this to happen include:

- ☒ I can believe for myself that my heavenly Father welcomes and embraces me when I repent, so that I lead my family in willing, joyful repentance.

- ☐ I can repent of my fears in disciplining my child . . .
    - ☒ fear of losing respect or control
    - ☒ fear of losing the battle
    - ☐ fear of being exposed as a poor parent
    - ☐ fear that I'm somehow ruining my child

. . . and engage in loving discipline because . . .

- ☒ I trust God to be the one who "builds the house."
- ☒ I trust God to use even my failures and sins to teach my child and me.
- ☒ I trust God to love me unendingly even though I'm often a failure.

- ☐ I can repent of the **selfish pride** that comes with disciplining my child . . .
    - ☒ pride in being able to handle the situation
    - ☒ pride in having children who respect and obey me
    - ☐ pride in doing discipline in the proper, biblical way

. . . and be humble in discipline, not having to prove myself, because . . .

- ☒ I know my righteousness comes from belonging to Jesus, not being a good parent.
- ☒ I know that I too am being disciplined by a wise Father who deeply loves me.
- ☒ I know that the Holy Spirit, not me, brings change to my child's heart.

- ☐ Other: _____

_____

(If your discussion would be helped by more thoughts on how looking to Jesus in the gospel will help both you and your child become more obedient to God, see the Conclusion to this study guide, on page 104.)

WRAP-UP AND PRAYER *10 minutes*

Even if we were perfectly loving and always encouraging with the gospel when correcting our children, we still would not have the power to transform their hearts. That is the Holy Spirit's work, not ours. So if this lesson reminded you of the many times you've failed with your children, or that your children seem hardened against discipline, resist the urge to respond with:

- Discouragement
- Defensiveness
- Denial
- Determination to do better

All of those are signs that we are depending on ourselves. Let's practice *faith in God* instead, through prayer. We have a loving Father who cares for us and our children. Pray together to him. Ask him to do what only he can: make your children willing to be corrected. Ask him to help you too, to become more gospel-centered in your discipline.

5

PARENTING THROUGH PRAYER

BIG IDEA

Because gospel parenting is about faith in God, prayer is a central part of it. Despite the many ways parenting proves that we need to pray, often we still neglect it. Perhaps we've become discouraged about prayer, or we feel unworthy, or we imagine that we're capable of handling things on our own. But prayer is the greatest parenting resource in the world, and it is freely available to us who believe in Jesus. We can learn to surrender our children to God in prayer, trusting his wise and compassionate care.

BIBLE CONVERSATION *15 minutes*

Prayer is at the core of faith in God, so the Bible says much about it. Let's look at a few passages that tell us some prayer basics.

(1) **Read Psalm 145:18–19.** According to these verses, what is God's response to prayer? List some of his qualities.

(2) **Read Philippians 4:6–7.** What qualities are found in a believer who prays? List these also.

(3) James warns that when we pray selfishly instead of surrendering to God's will, we don't get what we ask. "You ask and do not receive, because you ask wrongly, to spend it on your passions. . . . Humble yourselves before the Lord, and he will exalt you" (James 4:3, 10). It's hard to stay godly-minded in prayer, but **read Romans 8:26–28.** What help do we have when we struggle to pray as we ought? What assurance do we have that God will use even our broken prayers for our good?

****

Prayer should be one of the great encouragements in our parenting. So why does it sometimes feel like a burden instead? In the following article, Jack explains why he often finds it hard to pray. (Take turns reading the article aloud, switching readers at the paragraph breaks.)

BECOMING A PRAYING PARENT

10 minutes

We hope that these lessons have encouraged you so far, but it's entirely possible, if you are like us, that they also have been challenging. It's not easy to be reminded that you ought to repent quickly, consistently teach faith, and be more loving in discipline. Perhaps this study has exposed gaps in your parenting you'd rather ignore. Parenting is an overwhelming task anyway, but now you have more to do! It all adds up to the uncomfortable feeling of being needy.

When we feel needy, our natural reaction is to either resist feeling needy or let our needs discourage us. So this is an excellent time to study prayer, because Jesus taught a different way to deal with our needs: go to him in prayer. When his disciples asked him to teach them to pray, he told them an odd story of a man who had no choice but to bang on his neighbor's door in the middle of the night for bread (Luke 11:5–10). The point Jesus was making is that our needs keep us asking, seeking, and knocking, and that God will answer with himself—the gift of his Spirit (v. 13). It's good that parenting makes us feel needy, because our need should lead us to pray. It should bring us near to our Father, whose power and love will do far more for our children than we can imagine.

Perhaps, you know this and still struggle to pray. I'm that way. I know I *should* pray, but often I don't *want* to pray. Instead I get stuck in frustration or discouragement. And because my prayer life is weak I also feel condemned when I think about prayer, which just makes prayer even harder. Having struggled with this for years and seen some slow growth in my desire to pray, I've learned that the Bible encourages us to pray by pointing us to Jesus. To become praying parents, we need to see him better in at least three ways.

First, *when we feel condemned* **we must see what privileges we have in Jesus.** A slow-to-pray parent like me really is both foolish and sinful. Yet I must never think my bad track record disqualifies me from asking absolutely anything from God and receiving what's best. I pray *in Christ*, so I always have forgiven-of-my-sin access to my Father (Hebrews 10:19–22), the right to approach him as one who shares in Jesus's inheritance (Romans 8:15–17), and help from the Holy Spirit (Romans 8:26–27). That's right; as one who's lousy at prayer I have help, not condemnation, from God! The Spirit knows I struggle. He's there to pray *with me*. I can go to the Father at any time, with all of my thoughts and concerns, no matter how unworthy I'm feeling.

Second, *when we don't feel needy* **we must believe that Jesus's power is better than what we can do for ourselves.** I personally tend to be the got-it-handled type of parent. When parenting problems arise, I do my best to solve them. If I can't solve them, I either try harder or decide to ignore them. Turning to God is a distant, third choice I seldom employ. Just this week my wife and I were dealing with a discipline issue and she suggested we pray for our kids (it's usually her idea). I knew she was right, but part of me was also thinking, *Don't you think I can handle it?*

That was a sign of weak faith in God (and my pride!). I prefer *my* strength to trusting *his* strength. But our Savior is Lord of all! Whenever I imagine I'm the strong one in my family, and neglect prayer, I'm actually being the weak link. I need to stop being self-sufficient, and start depending on God's real power to change hearts and bring good out of sins and mistakes.

Third, *when we feel discouraged* **we must realize how kind Jesus is to those who call on him.** Sometimes I stop praying because I don't trust it to "work" or because I don't think God will answer the way I'd like. When prayer doesn't quickly give me the results I want, I give up on God and spend my time worrying or withdrawing instead. I fail to trust that however God answers my prayer, he surely will show me the same dazzling kindness Jesus showed throughout the Gospels. Jesus has unmatched compassion on everyone who comes to him begging and exhausted, in true surrender.

The Bible's account of Hannah is a great illustration of surrender through prayer. Hannah started with a deep need: she wasn't able to have a child. Her praying was so intense that she had to explain, "I was pouring out my soul to the LORD. . . . I was praying out of my great anguish and grief" (1 Samuel 1:15–16 NIV). Hannah had prayed before, but this time her prayer for a child included wholehearted surrender: "I will give him to the LORD for all the days of his life" (v. 11 NIV). Even before God gave her a child, Hannah felt peace "and her face was no longer downcast" (v. 18 NIV). Perhaps you too have poured out your heart to God about a child, with great anguish. Have you surrendered like Hannah, asking God to do what you can't—change their hearts to love him and others? We know our children well, but what a comfort it is to entrust them to the Father who knows them best.

Samuel, the son God gave Hannah, grew into a mighty prophet, and Hannah's prayers grew too. Before long, her anguish and self-concern gave way to praise for God's goodness and confidence in how he would use her family in his kingdom, for *his* purposes (1 Samuel 2). This is what prayer does. As we surrender our worries to God, we move from fear to faith, from grief to relief. Surrendering our concerns to God allows us to give up our urge for control and find rest instead in God's sure hand. Prayer is such sweet comfort!

For me, the value of these three blessings of prayer—privilege, strength, and comfort—have become even clearer since my mother's death. As I write this, it is exactly one month since her funeral. There's much about her I will miss, but perhaps the biggest loss is her prayers. She was a woman much like Hannah; weak in many ways but close to her strong

Savior. She prayed daily for me, my wife, and our children. No doubt her prayers for my family have advanced God's kingdom in yet-unseen but wonderful ways.

Who will pick up the slack now that she's gone? Who will be the family leader who knows personal weakness so keenly that the Father is never far away; who surrenders all to gain what is better; who prays humbly and repeatedly, and so brings God's blessings down like rain? Who, with the Spirit's kind help, will have that rare brand of strength that is received by calling steadily upon the King who is mighty to save? I want it to be me.

DISCUSSION *15 minutes*

(4) The article mentions three reasons why we might struggle to pray: discouragement, feeling self-sufficient instead of needy, and feeling unworthy. Which of these keeps you from praying? Or is there some other reason why you sometimes just don't want to pray?

(5) The article also mentions three gospel encouragements to pray: the compassion of Jesus, the power of Jesus, and the privilege of prayer because of Jesus. What about Jesus most encourages you to pray?

EXERCISE

PRAYING THE LORD'S PRAYER FOR YOUR FAMILY

25 minutes

We can use the Lord's Prayer (Matthew 6:9–13) as a foundation for praying for our children. It reminds us of the deep needs we have and gives us a pattern for praying about them.

Read each line, then jot down or share a brief prayer thought for your family that fits that line. Finish by briefly praying through each item. (NOTE: If your group is large, you might want to split into smaller groups of 2–4 people for this exercise, so that everyone has time to share and pray with the group.)

Our Father in heaven, hallowed be your name.

How has God shown your family his fatherly love and care?

PRAYER: Thank or praise God for this care.

Your kingdom come, your will be done, on earth as it is in heaven.

How might your family (children included) be involved in doing God's will or serving his kingdom?

PRAYER: Pray for God to help your family as you serve his kingdom this way—OR ask him to show your family how you can serve.

Give us this day our daily bread.

What is a current need your children face?

PRAYER: Ask God to meet this need.

Forgive us our debts, as we also have forgiven our debtors.

What sin have *you* contributed to your family? How have you sinned against your children and need to reconcile with them?

PRAYER: Confess your sin to God and ask his forgiveness. Also ask his help in family reconciliation.

Lead us not into temptation, but deliver us from evil.

What is a way your children are tempted to sin—OR what evils threaten to harm them?

PRAYER: Ask God to help your children resist that sin—OR to protect your children from that evil.

WRAP-UP *5 minutes*

The prayers brought up in the exercise are just some of those that flow naturally from praying through the Lord's Prayer (more ideas are in the leader's notes for this lesson, on page 118 in the back of this study guide). Consider using the Lord's Prayer as an ongoing guide this week to help you pray for your children. Particularly when you feel desperate or needy in your parenting this week, let that be a reminder from God to come to him.

6

WHEN YOUR CHILD DISAPPOINTS YOU

BIG IDEA

Despite our best efforts to love and to teach them, sometimes our children disappoint us. They embrace certain sins and show little interest in repenting, or they may even abandon faith in Jesus altogether. It helps to realize that *all* of God's children have, at one time, been wayward. We've all been disloyal to our Father and needed saving from sin, and he has responded to our betrayal with tender love. This gives us hope for our children—hope in God!—and it also helps us to respond to them out of love rather than getting stuck in anger and fear.

BIBLE CONVERSATION *15 minutes*

The prophet Hosea told how God loved his people from the time they were an infant nation, saving them out of Egypt and providing every good thing, only to have those people turn their backs on him. **Read Hosea 11:1–4.**

(1) What imagery does God use to describe himself as a Father? What fatherly love and care has he given?

(2) How did the people respond to God's fatherly love?

(3) God was angry with the people and determined to apply hard consequences, but did not destroy them. **Read verses 8–9.** What is it about God that keeps him from destroying the wayward people?

(4) If God's approach to his children is a model for us, how might we deal with our children when they disappoint us?

****

The book of Matthew tells us that the ache described in Hosea 11 was pointing ahead to Jesus (Matthew 2:15). The gospel is the answer to disappointing children! Read the following article from Rose Marie together. (Take turns reading it aloud, switching readers at the paragraph breaks.)

lesson

ARTICLE

HOW GOD PARENTS HIS WAYWARD CHILDREN

10 minutes

As parents we really don't expect to be disappointed. We might know intellectually that, just like us, our children are sinners who need a Savior, but we still struggle with surprise, frustration, fear, guilt, failure, and discouragement when we see our children make bad choices and act in ways that hurt themselves and others. When your children fail, when your hopes and dreams for them are crumbling before your eyes, how do you help them? How do you help yourself?

It's good to remember that our perfect heavenly Father also has wayward children. Actually *all* of his children, just like ours, have headed in the wrong direction. So he understands your sorrow. Listen to his heart for his people from Isaiah 5. "What more was there to do for my vineyard that I have not done in it? When I looked for it to yield grapes, why did it yield wild grapes?" (v. 4). This makes us think of Jesus's lament for his people in Jerusalem. "How often would I have gathered your children together as a hen gathers her brood under her wings, and you were not willing!" (Matthew 23:37).

Do you hear the sorrow? Do you see how Jesus, too, ached for those he had created, nurtured, and loved? Your friends or your church may not fully understand what you feel, but Jesus surely does! More than that, he's the solution. Right on the heels of the wayward children in

Isaiah comes the promise of a Son who will not disappoint: "to us a son is given" (Isaiah 9:6). Jesus never failed his Father or took a single step in the wrong direction. He obeyed perfectly and then gave his own life to bring peace, healing, and hope to all who have rejected God.

In my experience, we have to start with that truth—the good news that we have a Savior and that he understands—before we can see clearly how to help our children. Because as our children struggle, we struggle too. We lose hope. We feel shame. We wonder if God hears our cries for help. So before you consider how to respond to your child, go to your God who understands your sadness and ask for mercy and help. Then, remember the great truths of our faith: our Father in heaven is in charge of all things, his plans are good, he hears our cries for mercy, and our sins and our child's sins do not stop his love. Remember that he who did not spare his own Son will also freely give us all things and that nothing can separate us from the love of God in Christ Jesus. Take the time to read Romans 8:26–37 and pray specifically that the Spirit will give you God's perspective on your family.

When we see a child's sin, it's easy to rush in with anger, defensiveness, blame, and quick solutions. But instead of responding out of emotion, first bring your own heart to God. Do you harbor unbelief? Anger? Unforgiveness? Blame? Because of the cross of Christ, forgiveness is always available for both parent and child (1 John 1:9–10). Often our children's struggles are humbling to us. Perhaps we have taken pride in our parenting or in their accomplishments, but now we see clearly that we are helpless to change them. There is grace for the humble, and as we draw near to God, he will draw near to us with wisdom and help (James 4:6–8).

Also consider how you might need to forgive your child. You cannot move forward in your relationship with God or with your child unless you forgive. Perhaps you have a long list. Bring that list to your heavenly Father and ask him to show you how much grace you have been given, so that you have grace to spare for your child.

As the Spirit shows us our sins, assures us of God's love, and gives us an attitude of forgiveness, we can approach our struggling child in a new way. Instead of shouting, tears, recriminations, or cold withdrawal, we can talk with our child the way God approached his disappointing children in the Garden of Eden. When Adam and Eve sinned, God didn't come thundering at them; he asked a few simple questions: *Where are you? Who told you that you were naked? Have you eaten of the tree I commanded you not to eat? What is this you have done?* (Genesis 3:9–13). Starting with questions gives the Spirit the opportunity to reach your child's heart and gives you the opportunity to understand what your child might have been thinking (or not thinking!) and what desires led to the choices that were made.

Of course, there are always consequences for wrong choices, but you can apply those consequences (or watch as their choices carry their own consequences) out of love and forgiveness instead of anger and disappointment. Adam and Eve did experience terrible consequences, but God's love for them didn't fail and he promised right then and there to give them a Savior who would undo the evil that they had done (Genesis 3:18).

The temptation for us is to try to play God in our children's lives—to somehow manipulate our children into making good choices by using the correct discipline, saying the right words, getting them to come to church, or hear a dynamic speaker. Instead, why not let God do what he does best and reveal himself as you surrender and pray? Express your faith in love, and trust God to do the work you can't in your children's lives. During those hard years when our daughter left the faith, our praying became more centered on asking God to advance his kingdom and do his will instead of our own. And because God always moves toward us, we kept moving toward her, always including her in our lives and our plans, even as she tried to stay as far away from us as possible.

Of course we wanted her to change, but as we prayed the Spirit made us willing to wait for God to work in his way and time. He had a story for her also. All along he was planning to include her in his story and to add many others as well. And we had front row seats to what he was doing as we prayed, watched, loved, and waited for him to bring her into his kingdom. He not only brought her to faith, but also her live-in boyfriend, Angelo. After they married, he became a pastor, and they moved in with us and raised their family in our home. Today we still live, work, and pray together for God's kingdom to come and his will to be done. What God has done is truly far more than I could have asked or imagined! I can't say what result God has in store for you, but I do know he will do more than you could ask or imagine for your family too.

DISCUSSION *15 minutes*

(5) The article mentioned several emotions that tend to well up in us when our children make bad choices that hurt themselves or us: anger, fear, sadness, discouragement, guilt, and an urge to assign blame. Which ones most fit the way you tend to respond?

(6) Have your responses tended to be attempts to manipulate your child, or have you turned in faith to God? Give some examples.

(7) The article says, "It's good to remember that our perfect heavenly Father also has wayward children." How might remembering this help us as we parent our own wayward children?

lesson

EXERCISE

WAYS TO RESPOND TO A WAYWARD CHILD

20 minutes

Instead of just responding with anger and fear when our children misbehave, we can talk with them in ways that invite gospel repentance. This kind of dialogue fits a pattern God uses in the Bible.

> *Example:* When Adam and Eve first sinned, God called out to them and asked them about it. Rather than pushing them away, he invited them to engage him about their sin and he gave them an opportunity to confess and repent. "The man and his wife hid themselves from the presence of the LORD God among the trees of the garden. But the LORD God called to the man and said to him, 'Where are you?' And he said, 'I heard the sound of you in the garden, and I was afraid, because I was naked, and I hid myself.' He said, 'Who told you that you were naked? Have you eaten of the tree of which I commanded you not to eat?'" (Genesis 3:8–11).

Now think of a situation in which your children failed to behave as you wanted. Imagine your approach including some of the following strategies. None of them come easily for us, but pick a few you'd like to work on. Talk about how practicing these things would look different from the anger, fear, confusion, or disappointment we typically express when our children disappoint us.

Pause and pray. Before confronting your child, bring your heart to God. Ask yourself if your anger is selfish or if you harbor any unbelief, unforgiveness, or blame. Ask the Holy Spirit for a calm heart that can set such things aside and think clearly while listening.

Bring clarity. Ask questions that help your child organize thoughts and feelings in a way that lets you understand your child's struggle.

Questions that bring clarity:

- Tell me what happened.
- I would like to understand better what you are saying. Can you tell me what you mean by . . . ?
- How do you feel about . . . ?
- Tell me more about . . . ?
- What did you mean when you said . . . ?

Questions that DON'T bring clarity:

- What were you thinking!?
- How could you!?

Invite discussion. Explore beneath the surface. See if you and your child can identify what the child fears or is trusting for happiness—what's causing the troublesome behavior. You might unearth deep sin in your child's life, but resist the urge to be accusing. You want your child to share feelings, and even sins, openly and without worry of a scolding from a fellow sinner (you).

Questions that invite discussion:

- What were you afraid would happen if you didn't. . . ?
- Why does . . . make you feel happy (or safe)?

Questions/statements that DON'T invite discussion:

- You know the right thing to do, why can't you just do it?
- You know it's a sin! Just stop doing it!!

Speak the gospel. Talk often and naturally about the love of the Father for sinners who turn to him. Make sure your child knows that even if you have trouble forgiving or controlling *your* anger, the Father always forgives those who trust in Jesus. Speak humbly of your own sin and how you're forgiven.

Pray again. Don't just pray before speaking with your child; also pray during and after. Try to spend at least as much time talking about the situation to your heavenly Father as you do talking to your child. Believe that there's even more power in the talks you have with God than in the very best ones you might have with your child.

WRAP-UP AND PRAYER *10 minutes*

As you close, pray specifically for the hearts of your children. No amount of just-right questioning or gospel talk will melt their hearts unless the Holy Spirit does *his* work in them. So free yourself of that burden and let him carry it, through prayer.

lesson

7

ADVENTURES IN KINGDOM WORK

BIG IDEA

If we think our job as parents is merely to produce well-raised children, we are missing a spectacular wonder—that all who believe in Jesus are part of his kingdom and destined to rule with him. So one of the greatest joys of parenting is introducing our children to the thrill of kingdom work: building up the church, helping those in need, telling the good news of Jesus; pushing back against sin, death, and sadness everywhere as Christ reclaims his world and rescues his people. Instead of teaching our children to live for the emptiness of personal success, comfort, and/or approval, we invite them into a rich, meaningful life that counts for eternity.

BIBLE CONVERSATION *15 minutes*

(1) Jesus inaugurated his kingdom during his ministry on earth. **Read Matthew 9:35–38.** List the various aspects of his kingdom work. How might you generally describe the work?

(2) Jesus says he is looking for others to join in these aspects of his work. How might you describe the type of workers needed? What spiritual characteristics will they share with Jesus?

(3) How might this kingdom work compare to other work we typically do in the world?

(4) **Read Matthew 6:19–21.** How does this teaching from Jesus add to the appeal of service in his kingdom?

＊＊＊＊

Service in Christ's kingdom isn't just an individual thing—we do it together. And our families are an integral part of this work! In the following article, Rose Marie explains how this can happen. (Take turns reading the article aloud, switching readers at the paragraph breaks.)

lesson

ARTICLE

BRINGING YOUR FAMILY ON A REAL ADVENTURE

10 minutes

Living close to the Pacific Ocean, with the towering mountains behind us and the stately Redwoods just a day's drive away, instilled in us a sense of wonder about the world God made. We naturally shared that sense of wonder with our children. We took them on walks and named each tree we passed, watched the changing seasons, and pointed out each spectacular sunset. What we loved best we communicated easily and without effort to our family.

Take a moment and think about some of the things you love and how you have shared them with your family. Not hard at all, right? Books, sports, camping—whatever we like to do, we usually do in front of our children and with them as well. So sharing with your family about God's kingdom and bringing them with you on kingdom adventures starts with you. Does being a part of the greatest rescue mission in history fill you with wonder and excitement? Or does it feel like taking God's call seriously will just add to your already too long to-do list?

If you find yourself saying yes to that last question (as I certainly have!), then before you think about how to involve your family in God's kingdom, you probably need to consider whether you have lost your sense of wonder and joy at being accepted, forgiven, and brought into God's kingdom as his dearly loved child. Think back to when you first became a Christian, or anytime that you were full of joy because Jesus paid it all and did it all. Go back to the basics of remembering how broken you are by sin, how much God loves you, and how he sent his own Son to die for you. Ask for the Spirit to remind you of how much you have in Christ, so you can again be full of wonder in what Jesus has done and is doing for you.

In Revelation 2, Jesus speaks to the church at Ephesus. He commends them because they have worked hard, been faithful, and endured much. But there is one problem: they "abandoned the love they had at first" (Revelation 2:4). If Jesus isn't our first love, our children will certainly notice. But they will also notice when we repent for drifting away from our love for God. And love for God always overflows into caring for those around us. You can't change your child's heart or instill in them a love for God, but you can certainly let them see your love for God expressed in acts of love that bring God's kingdom to earth in your family, your neighborhood, your church, your city, and other countries.

Each of us has a role in Jesus's parting command to his disciples to take the gospel everywhere (Matthew 28:18–20). No one sits on the sidelines in God's kingdom. God needs his people to be everywhere, in every sphere of life sharing their faith and participating with the Spirit as Christ's church makes disciples. So, of course, this is your family's core calling as well. It doesn't mean that every Christian family does the same things or lives their kingdom calling in the same way. Quite the opposite. Each individual and each family will be a part of God's kingdom in a way that reflects their unique circumstances, season of life, and gifts. But there are some overarching principles to keep in mind as you take your family on a kingdom adventure.

1. Make sure your family understands the story of God's kingdom. Look together at Genesis 12:1–3. Teach your children the amazing story of the God who makes promises and keeps them. Point out to them that we are still living out God's promises to Abraham today as the followers of Christ grow into a family more numerous than the stars in the sky or the sand on the seashore.

2. How did you become a Christian? Do your children know that story? Share with them how God called you into his kingdom and how you are still part of his kingdom today (1 Peter 3:15).

3. Teach your children that the gospel is growing and bearing fruit all over the world (Colossians 1:5–6). Look for ways you can see God's kingdom changing the world. Talk about current events from a kingdom perspective. Get to know a missionary family and hear what they have to say about the kingdom of God in their part of the world.

4. Pray with your child for the needs of neighbors, friends, and relatives.

5. Reach out with your family to the needy people in your neighborhood, school, and church. Make sure this also includes those who are not part of your church community. If you make a meal, let your children be a part of that. Look for ways to help others that your family can do together.

6. Reach out with your family to needy people farther away—in your city, your country, and across the world.

As you go on a kingdom adventure with your family, don't forget how Jesus ended his parting words to his disciples. He said, "I am with you always, to the end of the age" (Matthew 28:20). The disciples weren't given an impossible task to complete on their own. The King of the universe, who holds all authority in heaven and earth, promised to be with them until the very end. That promise is for you and your family too. What Jesus calls you to do, he helps you to do. Live your love for him and he will be right beside you, leading, guiding, helping, and doing what you can't—changing the hearts of those with whom you share the good news of the kingdom.

DISCUSSION *15 minutes*

(5) Looking at the list from the article, what sort of thing do you feel encouraged to do to engage your family in kingdom work?

(6) Think of a way the gospel has encouraged you recently. If you told your children about it, how might it help them understand or get excited about kingdom work?

(7) How should Jesus's promise that he is with us always make kingdom work different for you than if you were to approach it on your own?

lesson

EXERCISE

START THE ADVENTURE

20 minutes

Getting involved (or more involved) in kingdom work isn't just about deciding to do something. Our families learn to love kingdom service as we practice believing the gospel.

- As we get honest about our sin, we become *humble* servants.
- As we learn to treasure Christ's love for us, we become *compassionate* servants.
- As we practice putting our hope in Jesus, we become servants who are *confident in Christ*.

This exercise will help you brainstorm about ways your family might engage in kingdom adventures—both how to serve Jesus and how to nurture the humility, compassion, and confidence that make it enjoyable. For each category, pick a thought or two and complete the sentence. Then share what you're thinking. The prayer notes will guide your prayer at the end of this lesson.

Identify roadblocks. What keeps you from considering kingdom work or engaging in it with your family?

PRESSURE: Instead of joy, when I think about serving our church or reaching out to others for the sake of Jesus, I feel pressured or guilty because _____.

MISPLACED PRIORITIES: I don't think my family has time for kingdom service because we're too busy with _____ . It consumes us.

COLDNESS: I care more about my own _____ than other people's _____ .

INSECURITY: The idea of doing kingdom work with my children makes me uncomfortable because _____ .

FEAR: I'll do anything except _____ , because I'm scared of _____ .

FEAR OF FAILURE: If I tried to get my children to _____ , I'm scared they would _____ .

Then pray about the roadblocks.

- Pray that God would humble you.
- Pray you would be aware of your sins and failings and grateful to Jesus for all he's done for you, giving you compassion for others.
- Pray for God to help you see his unconditional love for you, freeing you from concerns about how you look or how well you perform.

Set a foundation. What could you do regularly with your children to build a life that finds kingdom service appealing and exciting?

I could tell my children about God's work in my own life when I _____ .

We could have a family time to learn about Jesus and celebrate the gospel by _____daily/weekly.

I could talk with my children about _____ (remember questions that invite discussion from our last lesson).

I could set a tone in our home that's sin-aware, quick to repent, and grateful for Jesus, by freely talking about my own struggles to _____ .

Our family could learn more about God's work in _____ .

We could go to _____ to see what God is doing there.

Then pray for a foundation.

- Pray that God would help you to see the urgency and the exciting privilege of kingdom work.
- Pray for passion about seeing a specific part of God's kingdom grow.
- Pray that you would be able to model both humility and delight in Jesus for your children, and that he would bless them with those same qualities.
- Pray for a home where sin, forgiveness, and Jesus are discussed openly and with encouragement.

Start an adventure. What action might your family take to be actively involved in kingdom work?

Our family could pray regularly for _____ .

We could serve our church by _____ .

We could befriend someone in town who is _____ .

We could go along with _____ who is already serving by _____ .

We could go to _____ to help out by _____ .

We could support the kingdom work of _____ by doing _____ from our home.

Then pray for a good start.

- Pray that God would lead you to good ways to serve Christ's kingdom.
- Pray for wisdom to lead your family well.
- Pray for willingness and courage to answer Christ's call even amid uncertainties or when you aren't sure what idea is best.

WRAP-UP AND PRAYER *10 minutes*

Use the prayer notes at the end of each category in the exercise to guide your closing prayer time.

8

WALKING WITH YOUR FAMILY THROUGH SUFFERING

BIG IDEA

No family can escape suffering in this world. Walking with our children *through* suffering, while keeping our eyes and theirs fixed on Jesus, is an important part of gospel-centered parenting. The Bible teaches that Jesus has great compassion for us and is with us when we suffer. More than that, he entered into human suffering to bear our worst griefs for us. Even more, he redeems what suffering remains and uses it to work good in our lives and bring glory to God. Most of all, he always gives us himself and his love no matter what we may suffer, and one day he will end our suffering forever. None of this makes suffering easy at the moment, but it does mean that our pain is accompanied by faith, not hopelessness.

NOTE TO GROUPS: For Christians, suffering brings varied feelings. As you discuss suffering, be careful not to scold others if they don't share your feelings about it.

- <u>Don't</u> suppress sadness. (Don't say, "You shouldn't be sad; you should have joy in Jesus.")
- <u>Don't</u> suppress hopefulness either. (Don't say, "It's insensitive to keep mentioning how God will make things better.")

Both sadness and hopefulness are actually highly appropriate. Of all people, Christians can be *most saddened* by suffering, knowing how good life ought to be, and also *most hopeful* in suffering, knowing God is with us and has a loving plan.

BIBLE CONVERSATION *15 minutes*

John 9 tells the story of Jesus's encounter with a man born blind and his parents. Have someone **read John 9:1–7** aloud.

(1) The blind man and his parents must have suffered much. According to Jesus, what was the purpose behind that suffering?

(2) How does Jesus's answer make you feel about suffering? What's encouraging about his answer? Is there anything that feels insensitive or incomplete about it?

As the story in John 9 progresses, the blind man tells what Jesus did for him, and Jesus's enemies cast the blind man out of the synagogue (like being expelled from church) for his testimony. **Read John 9:35–39** to see what Jesus did then.

(3) What evidence do you see of Jesus's compassion for the blind man— both while the man was still blind and later when he was persecuted? List several things that Jesus did for him, both in the latter part of the story and at the beginning.

(4) Why does it matter that this account both teaches the truth that the family's suffering was for good and also shows Jesus's compassion and care? (The man came to faith! Others saw a sign of Jesus's power and compassion. Some who saw were challenged about their own blindness.)

****

One of the most important things we can teach our children is how to deal with suffering. In this article, Jack shares what he's learned from parents who did that job well. (Take turns reading the article aloud, switching readers at the paragraph breaks.)

lesson

ARTICLE

LOOKING TO JESUS IN THE HARDEST TIMES

10 minutes

A girl comes home in tears from her first day at middle school, devastated because her best friend will have nothing to do with her. A high school basketball star collapses on the court with a knee injury, ending both his season and his chance for a scholarship. A ten-year-old learns her parents are getting divorced. A five-year-old is told his mother is dying of cancer. These things are as heartbreaking to us parents as they are to our children. Surely we cry with our kids when they happen. But we also hope that amid such suffering our children *will not lose faith*. We know that it is faith in Jesus's love for us that sustains us through the best of times and the worst of times.

I've known families who have gone through all those kinds of suffering, and perhaps you have too. The Bible tells us we cannot avoid suffering in this life. God is with us *through* suffering, but he won't rescue us *from* suffering until we reach heaven. That's an important truth to teach our children.

Expecting suffering doesn't make it easy. Suffering tests our faith, and it tests the faith of our children. How do we teach our children to live by faith through suffering? We start by reminding ourselves and them that Jesus is our Emmanuel, our God who is with us. He is "a man of sorrows and acquainted with grief" (Isaiah 53:3). The God who is with us understands every kind of suffering. So we can go to him and encourage our children to go to him with our suffering—no matter what it is.

We do grieve, deeply. Our children will grieve deeply. But, as Jesus did, we also look through the pain to our heavenly Father. You can encourage your child to cry out his or her questions, anger, and hurt to him (Psalm 22). Going to God with all of our sorrows is an act of faith. It means we see that our suffering is ultimately in *his* hands. Although evil powers, the world's brokenness, and our own sin all bring suffering, God is King over all those forces! He only allows suffering that ultimately works good for us behind the scenes. Since he's both Almighty God and our good Father, it means we will not "grieve as others do who have no hope" (1 Thessalonians 4:13).

The story of Ruth is an example of this. It begins with a family forced by famine out of their homeland to Moab, a godless country where the husband and his two sons die. The wife Naomi, bereft of her husband and sons, cries, "The Almighty has dealt very bitterly with me" (Ruth 1:20). She wisely directs her complaint at the One who also provides hope. God did have a plan behind her hard circumstances, but it took more than ten years from the time her suffering began before she got the first glimpse of his purposes in the midst of her suffering. That's when he used the situation to work faith in her daughter-in-law Ruth, to provide Ruth with a godly husband, and to give Naomi a grandson.

But we mustn't stop there. The book ends with a zinger that Naomi and Ruth never realized *their entire lives*. Ruth's baby became the grandfather of the great King David. So God used the suffering in their family to richly bless their entire nation—although they never knew it. What's more, the rest of the Bible shows how God used David's family to give birth to Jesus and save the whole world from sin! Even the author of Ruth never knew *that*. And when Jesus came, he himself suffered and by doing so showed the pure goodness of God more sweetly than ever before. Nothing is more love-soaked than the blood of the cross.

What about your family's suffering? What can you tell your kids? Well, in this life you may see very little of the good plan God has for you. But even if you have the joy of seeing some of God's plan unfold, surely the best is yet to come. You cannot conceive of the wonders God has in store for you and your children! So teach them that we "groan inwardly as we wait eagerly for adoption as sons, the redemption of our bodies" (Romans 8:23).

And while you wait, whether with little suffering or much, the very best thing about your life is that you belong to Jesus. Suffering will train you to realize that in him you have vast riches. The devil would like you to think an easy life is better than a life with God. But suffering shows us that nothing in this world will last. Your only dependable comfort is Jesus—both the future he promises and the friendship you have with him now, while you're suffering. Tell your kids that too.

Many years ago, when I was still a young teacher, I served in camp ministry. One summer, a little girl attending her first overnight camp had a bad case of homesickness. I knew her family, so it became my job to cheer her up. I tried every trick—games, friends, chocolate chip cookies—but nothing made her happy. Finally I asked her if I could pray for her. She gave me a huge grin and said yes, and she felt much better afterwards. I knew then that her parents were doing something right. They'd taught her that when we're sad we look to God.

A few months later, this girl and her family discovered that she had cancer. Surgeries, chemotherapy, and years of rehabilitation followed. The next time I saw her at camp she was a teenager, and despite all her treatments the cancer was still with her. I knew she and her family had been through deep suffering and the worst might still be ahead. So on the last day of camp, when we were writing personal messages on T-shirts the campers would take home with them, on her shirt I didn't scribble the typical line about what a cool kid she was. Instead I brashly wrote, "Always remember how God has been so very good to you!"

Right away I got nervous. What if she found my message insensitive or simplistic? But when I showed her what I'd written she rewarded me with that same grin I'd seen years before. That girl knew. She had learned that when every other pleasure of life is wrenched away, Jesus remains—and he is more precious, more caring, and more trustworthy than absolutely anything else. Good job, Mom and Dad!

DISCUSSION *15 minutes*

The article mentions three things to teach our children about suffering:

- God is with us through suffering but won't rescue us from suffering until heaven.
- We cannot fully imagine what wonders God has in store for us.
- The promises and friendship of Jesus are far better than an easy life.

(5) What other truths about Jesus and the gospel do you think are particularly important to teach our children as we walk with them through suffering? (NOTE: When you've thought of everything you can, this might be a time to peek at the leader's notes for this lesson, on page 125 in the back of this study guide.)

(6) If you can, share an example of a truth about Jesus and the gospel that was helpful to your family during a time of suffering.

(7) Think about what you know of how Jesus approached his own suffering and death. (Did he feel it strongly or suppress it? How did he engage others? How did he engage God?) What can you learn from him about how to act when suffering comes?

lesson

EXERCISE

HOW FAITH TRANSFORMS SUFFERING

20 minutes

Suffering not only compels us to look to Jesus; it also helps us understand our own hearts. We all have a gap between what we believe about Jesus and what we actually live out. Suffering trains us to live up to what we believe: that nothing is better than the love of Jesus and nothing we suffer can defeat that love. "Who shall separate us from the love of Christ? Shall tribulation, or distress, or persecution, or famine, or nakedness, or danger, or sword?" (Romans 8:35).

The hurts and strong feelings that come with suffering may lead us to act in ways that don't fit what we believe. Strong feelings themselves are not always wrong. For example, Jesus felt both anger and sadness when he encountered suffering. But when these feelings are not accompanied by faith, they can lead to behaviors like *blaming, fixing,* and *withdrawing*. See which feelings and behaviors you relate to in the following chart.

Common Responses to Suffering

BLAMING

You find someone to blame for the suffering that's happened to you or your children.

You may feel:
- **Angry.** You dream of the day when someone will pay for what's happened.
- **Judgmental.** You're eager to point out what others have done wrong or how they've betrayed you.
- **Guilty.** You blame yourself, or you blame your children for their own suffering.

You fail to feel:
- Compassionate
- Forgiving

You fail to live as one who believes that although evil may have a role in suffering, all suffering is in God's hands and he is using it for your good.

You fail to be humble and know that you too deserve judgment for many failures and betrayals but have received mercy from Jesus.

FIXING

You obsess over fixing the suffering and won't let others be accepting of it.

You may feel:
- **Scared.** You're fearful of suffering or worried it will make you look/feel like a failure.
- **Confused.** You can't understand why the suffering is happening or accept that it's happening to you.
- **Doubtful.** You wonder if God really is loving, wise, and in control, so you act as if your happiness (and others' happiness) depends on your own efforts.

You fail to feel:
- Content
- Sympathetic to those who grieve

You fail to live as one who believes that your greatest joy is found in God himself and what he gives you, not in your ability to avoid troubles.

You fail to rest in God and his love for you.

WITHDRAWING

You avoid dealing with the suffering and helping your children through it.

You may feel:
- **Afraid.** You're scared you'll mishandle suffering and you fear the pressure, awkwardness, or exposure of trying to help. You may be "freaked out" by it.
- **Sad.** You feel unable to help anyone because you're overwhelmed.
- **Self-pitying.** You can only see your suffering. You see no reason to think of others.
- **Bitter.** You get fed up with God and neglect your spiritual habits: prayer, worship, personal devotions, and meeting with fellow believers.

You fail to feel:
- Helpful
- Hopeful

You fail to live as one who believes that God is with you through suffering, caring deeply for you and helping you.

You fail to have hope in Jesus and the future he's planned for you.

Pick one or two behaviors or feelings from the chart that fit your experience with suffering, and share them with the group. Give an example if you can. NOTE: The feelings that come with suffering are complex, and your experience may not completely fit any of these categories. That's okay. Share the part that does fit.

Tell how your behaviors might change if you more consistently lived out what you believe about Jesus.

WRAP-UP AND PRAYER *10 minutes*

The faith we need to walk with our children through suffering is not conjured up by our own efforts. Rather, it is *received* from God. So finish by praying that God would help you have faith in him in the midst of suffering. If some in your group are going through a time of particular suffering, pray for them:

- That God would show them compassion
- That God would "sanctify their suffering" and use it to accomplish much good
- That God would give them faith to say, "My flesh and my heart may fail, but God is the strength of my heart and my portion forever" (Psalm 73:26).

9

SPIRITUAL WARFARE AND YOUR FAMILY

BIG IDEA

The Christian life is a battle. Although Jesus has saved us from sin, the fight against sin is not yet over. We and our children are threatened, every moment of every day, by evils both coming against us from the *outside* and welling up *inside* of us. Preparing our children for this battle, and teaching them to rely on their Savior as they fight alongside him, is one of our most important tasks as parents.

BIBLE CONVERSATION *15 minutes*

(1) **Read 1 John 2:15–17.** What is the alternative to loving the things of our heavenly Father? Does this threat come from *outside* of us or from the *inside*? Explain.

(2) Now read Paul's account of his personal battle with sin from **Romans 7:21–25.** Does this threat come from the outside or from inside of him? Give an example of situation in which you knew what was right and wanted to do right, but still gave in to another inward desire to do what was wrong.

(3) The temptation to sin is particularly dangerous because it has a personal, scheming force behind it. **Read Ephesians 6:10–17.** Looking at verses 10–12, list some words you might use to describe our adversary.

(4) Later we'll look in detail at the armor "pieces," but in general, what hope do we have to stand against the devil?

****

One way to think about the fight we're in is to summarize it as being against three evils:

1. The world
2. The flesh (the sinful nature that still affects us even after God has made us alive in Christ)
3. The devil

In this article, Rose Marie shares how she came to understand these dangers and the way we overcome them. (Take turns reading the article aloud.)

lesson

ARTICLE

YOUR FAMILY'S
REAL BATTLE

10 minutes

We might not easily connect the phrase "spiritual warfare" with family life. Perhaps it brings to mind fire and brimstone sermons or horror movies featuring exorcisms. But the Bible is clear that being Christians means we and our children enter into a fight against evil—in us, the world, and the devil.

This battle was not uppermost in our minds when my husband and I were parenting our children. But, like most parents, we certainly were interested in protecting them from what we identified as bad outside influences. So we circled the wagons around our five children—making sure that what they read and saw on TV, the friends they hung out with, and the school they attended all reflected Christian values.

There was nothing wrong with doing this. It was part of our calling as Christian parents to protect our children (although we might have gone a little too far in some areas!). But even in our going "too far," we hadn't really gone far enough, because we didn't take into account that evil was not just outside our family but was inside each of us. We each have hearts that are bent and broken by sin.

Satan's stronghold in this world started in the Garden of Eden. Adam and Eve had a perfect relationship, home, and job—really nothing to complain about! But Satan tempted them to eat the forbidden fruit; to question God's goodness and truthfulness and to lust after something better they might get for themselves. He told them, "You will not surely die. For God knows that when you eat of it your eyes will be opened, and you will be like God" (Genesis 3:4–5). Their desire for the *world* made their *flesh* sinful and enslaved them to the *devil*.

So the bad news is that evil is not just outside our families; it has a place in the self-centered hearts of both parents and children. But the good news is that Jesus lived, died, rose again, and gives us his Spirit to deliver us from the evil within and without. Understanding the battle we and our children face is important, but it's just as important to know that we are not left defenseless. Jesus has given us his Spirit who changes our hearts, convicts us of sin, shows us our need for a Savior, and gives us the power to turn from going our own way and to follow Jesus. We need his help. We must let our children see our need, and come alongside them when they're battling sin and show them where to turn. We cannot battle evil alone.

Our help is laid out for us in Ephesians 6. The armor of God by which we stand against the devil's schemes is simply Christ and all he does for us. The pieces point us to him.

- *Helmet of salvation:* We are saved by Jesus.
- *Breastplate of righteousness:* Jesus makes us right in God's eyes.
- *Belt of truth:* In Jesus we identify the lies we listen to and turn from them.
- *Gospel of peace:* The good news of Jesus, that our sins are forgiven and death is conquered, is our joyful message.

This is who we are in Jesus. It is our comfort, our strength, and our confidence when the devil tempts us.

The armor continues with the all-important equipment that connects us to Jesus—the *shield of faith*. Faith in Christ brings the power of God into the lives of parents and children and extinguishes all the flaming darts of the evil one. His fiery darts are no different today from those he tempted Eve with: "God is holding back something good from you."

"God cannot be trusted." "It is up to you to take charge." "You are alone." But instead of listening to him, we can identify those thoughts as lies from the pit of hell and help our children as well to see those lies for what they are. Then, by faith, we can come to God with no resources, no strength, no righteousness, and no wisdom other than his, and ask for the Spirit to fill us so that we will stand firm.

Then, covered head to toe by the goodness of Jesus, we go on the offensive. We take the *sword of the Spirit*, which is the Word of God, and pray at all times in the Spirit (Ephesians 6:17–18). When my husband and I first understood that as parents we could not protect our children from evil within and without, we were afraid and discouraged. But praying became a door of hope for us. By faith we believed that God's promise was for us and for our children. We stopped being afraid and trusted the Spirit to do in our family what we could not do. That freed us to love our children just as they were, without taking on the burden of change that only God could do.

As we prayed, we found that the kingdom of God really is a more powerful force than the kingdom of this world. Although we saw how weak we are in ourselves, we also saw that God's power is unstoppable. He did what we couldn't do—he changed the hearts of our children, and our hearts too. I still put on the armor of God and pray for God's kingdom to come and will to be done in me and my family. As we struggle with the world, the flesh, and the evil one, we don't lose hope because he who is in us is more powerful than he who is in the world (1 John 4:4).

DISCUSSION *10 minutes*

(5) Ephesians 6 says faith in Christ extinguishes the flaming darts of the evil one. What darts (lies or doubts about God's goodness) has the evil one hurled at you or your children recently? How do they threaten to keep you from living for God?

(6) How does the promise that he who is in us (God) is more powerful than he who is in the world (the devil) affect our daily parenting?

lesson

EXERCISE

USING THE ARMOR OF GOD

20 minutes

Since we are in a daily battle for our lives and the lives of our children, it helps to practice using the armor God gives us. We must take up the Word of God and believe it; strong in the truth, righteousness, salvation, peace, and faith that are ours in Christ.

To practice, discuss the following case study and how your family might use these pieces of "armor" to battle some common family sins.

Case Study: The Unfair Coach

THE SITUATION
Your child has played for a few years on a local sports team, and has seemed to play well. But this year the team has a new coach who, for no apparent reason, doesn't like your child. You've tried talking to the coach about this but he has little interest in listening. Then last week, the coach cut your child from the team. Your child was in tears, feeling hurt by not being able to play with the team and shame at being cut.

THE TEMPTATION
Your whole family is angry at the coach. You are tempted to hate him. Your instinct is to tell others what happened so that the coach looks bad and suffers. You dream of other ideas for revenge too, and you hope the coach has a lousy season and loses his job. You know Jesus taught

that you should love people—even your enemies—but the temptation to hate the coach is strong.

THE FIGHT

Focus on the temptation to hate. Using the armor of God, how do you as a family fight the (understandable) temptation to be hateful? For instance:

- RIGHTEOUSNESS: How could the righteousness you enjoy in Christ affect any shame felt over being cut from the team? *SAMPLE ANSWER: In Christ we enjoy acceptance with God. He sees us as righteous and helps us to act righteously by his standards. This becomes far more meaningful to us than how the world views us or how well we meet its standards.*
- TRUTH: What truth about the benefits of belonging to Christ vs. the benefits of the world might be helpful to study and remember?
- GOSPEL OF PEACE: How might the peace with God that you've received through the gospel affect your relationship with the coach?
- FAITH: What about God's goodness will be important to believe and trust?
- SALVATION: How does your salvation change the way you think about the wrong that's been done to your family?
- WORD OF GOD: What Bible passages might be good ones to read as a family in this situation? Why?
- PRAYER: What kind of prayer would be particularly helpful?

WRAP-UP AND PRAYER *15 minutes*

Pray together against the three enemies of the believer.

1. Pray for strength for your family to resist the enticements of the world.
2. Pray for victory over the temptations of the flesh (evil desires still inside you and your children).
3. Pray that the devil's schemes would be thwarted.

lesson

10

PERSEVERANCE AND HOPE

BIG IDEA

The daily, yearly, and lifelong pressures and concerns of parenting can exhaust us or even push us toward despair. One of our most important parenting tasks is simply to not give up. There will be times when our parenting looks like utter failure; when even if we are trusting God we can hardly bear to wait for him to make things better. At such times, God invites us to come to him in our frustrations (even our frustrations with *him*) and hear his promises anew. Nothing stabs more bitterly at the soul than the feeling that God has abandoned you, but nothing more sweetly restores hope than the reminder that he does love you.

BIBLE CONVERSATION *15 minutes*

Psalm 13 is a common kind of psalm called a *lament*. A lament expresses the feelings that come when life seems to be going very wrong. This psalm of David has three parts: it starts in anguish, progresses through prayer, and ends in hope. Have someone **read all of Psalm 13**.

(1) *Part 1: Anguish.* Describe how David's troubles feel to him in verses 1 and 2. We don't know what David's troubles were at this time, but think of a few parenting troubles that might lead a mom or dad to have the same kind of feelings.

(2) *Part 2: Prayer.* When life has so many problems, our only relief is to turn to God. In verse 3, what might David mean when he asks the Lord to light up his eyes?

(3) *Part 3: Hope.* Describe the change that takes place in David at the end of the psalm, after he has brought his troubles to God. What's different inside of him?

****

Psalm 13 shows that we can have deep, comforting faith even in the midst of frustration and uncertainty. In the following article, Rose Marie tells the story of her own experience with the question, "How long, O Lord?" (Take turns reading the article aloud, switching readers at the paragraph breaks.)

HOW LONG, O LORD?

10 minutes

Our daughter Barbara left faith and family when she was eighteen. Five years later she moved back home for a few months, but her journey away from God and us was not over. In her bedroom we left up a burlap banner her sister had made, with Barbara in mind, that simply said, "How long, O LORD?" (Psalm 13:1). Barbara looked at it when she moved in, rolled her eyes, and was soon moving out to live with yet another man. My husband and I looked at each other and wondered, "How long, O Lord?"

The question, "How long, O Lord?" is one that can be asked all through our parenting journey. We wonder:

- How long before my child sleeps through the night?
- How long before my child hears the word "No" and actually listens?
- How long before my teenager makes better choices?
- How long before _____ ?

(Fill in the blank with your own "How long, O Lord?")

The list goes on and on. At any stage of the parenting journey (which, by the way, is never over!), we can become discouraged by our children's struggles, and of course the temptation is to lose hope, to give up. In Dante's ancient classic, *Inferno,* the entrance to hell had these famous words written over it, "Abandon all hope ye who enter here." His definition of hell is a world with no hope. That certainly can be applied to parenting. Without hope, persevering through the ups and downs of parenting becomes a joyless slog.

So when your child is struggling, what do you put your hope in? As parents, what we really want is the assurance that our child will be safe, healthy, happy, productive, and successful. We want God to promise that! But God promises something so much better—his presence. Jesus came to this earth as Emmanuel, "God with us." God himself came to this earth, shared our sorrows, our struggles, our temptations, and then went to the cross to save us from sin and death.

When Jesus rose from the dead and ascended to heaven, he did not leave us to face life alone, on our own as orphans. Jesus knew we could not persevere in hope without him. So he promised to give us his Spirit: "I will ask the Father and he will give you another Helper, to be with you forever, even the Spirit of truth" (John 14:16–17). When the Spirit of God fills us, he pours into our hearts the assurance of God's love, and that fills us with hope despite our children's struggles (Romans 5:5).

- Instead of responding with despair when we see our sins and our children's sins, the Spirit reminds us that our God is merciful, forgiving, and kind to our children and us (Psalm 103:8–18).
- Instead of being filled with fear when our family encounters difficult circumstances, the Spirit reminds us that the hardest things are not outside of God's plan, but are part of his plan to bring good (Romans 8:28).
- When we are tempted to think we are the exact wrong parents for our children, the Spirit reminds us that God placed our children with us so they could know him (Acts 17:26–27).
- When we are tempted to think that our children will never turn toward God, the Spirit reminds us that God works in and through families (Acts 11:14; 16:31).
- When we are afraid that God has given up on us and our children, the Spirit reminds us that nothing can separate us from God's love (Romans 8:35–39).

These are the promises we pray for our children, asking the Spirit to do what we can't—fill our children's hearts with God's love and turn their hearts to him in faith. Often we don't know exactly what to pray for our child, but the Spirit takes our prayers and prays them with and for us, bringing our prayers right into the throne room of our heavenly Father. Are you too weak to pray for your child? Remember that "the Spirit helps us in our weakness. For we do not know what to pray for as we ought, but the Spirit himself intercedes for us with groanings too deep for words" (Romans 8:26). What a great exchange! We bring our weakness and the Spirit pleads for us.

Hanging that banner up wasn't meant to change Barbara (and really, in retrospect, leaving it up there for her to see might not have been the best parenting strategy), but it was an honest cry to God that arose from our family's concern for her. It was a human question seeking a divine answer—an answer from the one who knows the beginning from the end.

At the close of the Bible, the same Jesus who came to be with us as Emmanuel, and who gives us his Spirit, also answers the "how long?" question. He tells us, "Surely I am coming soon" (Revelation 22:20). This is not a timeline or a guarantee that things will turn out as we planned, but combined with "I am with you always" (Matthew 28:20) it is a great and precious promise. As we turn to God in faith, we can *always* look back and say that God has been with us through the ups and downs of parenting. And we can always look ahead knowing that one day—not too long now—he will end our frustration and bring us safely home. Then we will see clearly how God did work *all things* for the good of those who love him and are called according to his purposes (Romans 8:28).

DISCUSSION *10 minutes*

(4) Think of a time when your heart also cried out, "How long, O Lord?" How would or did you fill in the blank: How long before . . . ?

(5) What promises of God are an answer to the way you filled in that blank? What hope do you have because of Jesus?

lesson

EXERCISE

HOPE FOR EVERY DAY

25 minutes

Some of the lessons in this book may have led you to think, *How long, O Lord?* You may have thought it about your children's struggles, or perhaps you thought it when a lesson showed how much *you* still need to grow as a gospel-centered parent. In either case, "How long, O Lord" is a good cry of faith. It means you're turning to God for answers and help—both with your children's problems and your parenting.

For each lesson we've studied, notice the cry for help that may arise and a promise of hope that God gives. Pick one or two of the lessons and tell how they were particularly meaningful or eye-opening to you. How might you, like David, keep praying about those struggles or hopes?

LESSON 1: UNLESS THE LORD BUILDS THE HOUSE

How long, O Lord until I put aside my anxiety, stop being overbearing or controlling, and rest in you to care for my family?

Hope: Your Father not only protects your family; he gives faith to you. "He gives to his beloved sleep" (Psalm 127:2).

I need to keep praying for _____ .

LESSON 2: THE PARENT AS THE CHIEF REPENTER

How long, O Lord will I remain afraid to repent openly, in front of my children?

Hope: Repentance is attractive and shows kids the value of Jesus. "Create in me a clean heart, O God, and renew a right spirit within me. Then I will teach transgressors your ways, and sinners will return to you" (Psalm 51:10, 13).

I need to keep praying for _____ .

LESSON 3: TEACHING YOUR CHILD "ON THE WAY"

How long, O Lord will I struggle with the pressure and difficulty of sharing your Word with my children?

Hope: There's no formula, rather a whole life of natural teaching opportunities. "Talk of them when you sit in your house, and when you walk by the way" (Deuteronomy 6:7).

I need to keep praying for _____ .

LESSON 4: DISCIPLINE BY FAITH, NOT FRUSTRATION

How long, O Lord will my child's disobedience and my angry, resentful, or shaming response to it continue?

Hope: The gospel heals. It trains you to act out of love (because you've been loved!) rather than a need for order or respect. "We love because he first loved us" (1 John 4:19).

I need to keep praying for _____ .

LESSON 5: PARENTING THROUGH PRAYER

How long, O Lord until I become a parent who loves to pray and gladly says to God, "Your will be done"?

Hope: Prayer is not a burden God has placed on you, but part of his eagerness to bless you. "The LORD is near to all who call on him" (Psalm 145:18).

I need to keep praying for _____ .

LESSON 6: WHEN YOUR CHILD DISAPPOINTS YOU

How long, O Lord will my child live this way? I'm at a complete loss for what to do!

Hope: God is a tender Father who has much concern for wayward children—like you once were! "My compassion grows warm and tender" (Hosea 11:8).

I need to keep praying for _____ .

LESSON 7: ADVENTURES IN KINGDOM WORK

How long, O Lord until we feel free to live for your kingdom. I'm overwhelmed just getting my kids to all their activities!

Hope: You learn to love kingdom service as you learn to believe in the King. "Lay up for yourselves treasures in heaven, where neither moth nor rust destroys and where thieves do not break in and steal" (Matthew 6:20).

I need to keep praying for _____ .

LESSON 8: WALKING WITH YOUR FAMILY THROUGH SUFFERING

How long, O Lord! Words can't begin to express the gut-wrenching sorrow I feel in the midst of this struggle.

Hope: Jesus is with you when you suffer, full of compassion and planning good for you. "In all these things we are more than conquerors through him who loved us" (Romans 8:37).

I need to keep praying for _____ .

LESSON 9: SPIRITUAL WARFARE AND YOUR FAMILY

How long, O Lord will temptations be everywhere? We're tired of fighting them.

Hope: In Jesus, we have God's armor to stand against the devil's schemes. "Be strong in the Lord and in the strength of his might" (Ephesians 6:10).

I need to keep praying for _____ .

WRAP-UP AND PRAYER *10 minutes*

Use the prayer needs you picked out of the exercise to guide your closing prayer time.

CONCLUSION:

FIFTEEN REASONS TO TRAIN YOUR CHILD IN THE GOSPEL OF GRACE

The idea of parenting your children first of all by believing the gospel and teaching it to them may still seem odd to you. Especially when it comes to training your children, you may be wondering, *But don't I have to teach them to obey God?*

Yes, you do. Obedience to God is both commanded and a great joy, so you absolutely want to teach your children to obey. But first of all you *must* train in them the gospel. It's foundational.

One concern parents sometimes have is that putting the gospel first—especially stressing the absolute forgiveness and righteousness we already have in Christ—will make it sound to their children as if obeying God doesn't matter. Or parents worry that the strategy of fostering love for God by telling of his love for us will make their kids think they don't have to obey God unless they feel like it. Parents fear it all might lead to lax obedience.

Please don't worry. The Holy Spirit uses the gospel. To encourage you, here are fifteen reasons why teaching the gospel—teaching to the heart—will actually help your children to obey God better than if you merely tell them to obey. This list is adapted from a list in another Serge resource, *Show Them Jesus* by Jack Klumpenhower (New Growth Press, 2014).

1. Unless their hearts are in it, your kids won't be obeying God's most important law no matter what else they might manage to do. The great and first commandment is "Love the Lord your God with all your heart" (Matthew 22:37). So don't worry that gospel teaching is slack about obedience. When you help kids to obey gladly, in a lifestyle of heartfelt gratitude rather than under pressure, you're actually being very serious about God's commands. You're setting the bar high— where God sets it.

2. Unless good works spring from belief in Jesus, they aren't even actually *good*. Belief is so central that "whatever does not proceed from faith is sin" (Romans 14:23) and, "without faith it is impossible to please him" (Hebrews 11:6). When your kids learn about and believe the gracious blessings that are theirs in Jesus, they've laid the mandatory foundation for *true* obedience.

3. Obedience that's grounded in love will help your kids overcome how they feel at the moment. Obeying out of love isn't a wishy-washy thing that depends on feelings. There will be times your kids don't feel like obeying God. But if they love him they'll have a steady, underlying desire to obey him, even amid temptation and mixed feelings. That's the nature of love.

4. The worry that God's people might use grace as an excuse to sin reflects a too-small view of salvation and grace. If you only taught how God freely forgives us—then okay, grace might make your kids think they can sin as much as they like. But the salvation you'll be teaching them includes "a holy calling" (2 Timothy 1:9) and "the hope laid up for you in heaven" (Colossians 1:5). Kids gripped by such big grace have a taste of heaven and holiness that makes them hungry to live like holy, heaven-bound people now.

5. The idea that grace might let us get away with sin is not how reborn people should think. Romans 6:1–14 says an attitude that asks "How much can I get away with?" belongs to the old, worldly life. In Christ we're set free of that selfish motive, so you shouldn't pander to it by avoiding talk of God's grace. If your kids live by the avoid-punishment motive, they'll do the minimum to get by. You want to instill a love-for-Christ motive so that they'll do the most they can.

6. A strategy that starts with believing the gospel looks beyond surface sins to whole-self obedience. Unless your kids address their root unbelief and coldness toward God, any fight against sin they may undertake will have a lousy strategy. They'll ignore the heart and get nowhere, because "out of the abundance of the heart his mouth speaks" (Luke 6:45).

7. Your kids can't be consistent about godly living without love for God. By willpower they might resist a sin here and there on a good day or when you are watching. But most of the time their hearts win out— they serve what they love. Your kids only become consistently obedient when their sinful loves give way to a bigger love for God (1 John 2:15).

8. Your kids can't really obey God if they're unsure of his pleasure toward them. If they aren't first convinced God loves them, forever and unfailingly, everything they do for him will only be a scheme to impress him and try to earn or keep his love. That's manipulation, not obedience.

9. A focus on Jesus and his grace does not make God's commands seem unnecessary; instead it shows how they're both urgent and beautiful. All of Jesus's saving work and especially his sacrifice for sin increases our debt of love, compels us to be thankful, and shows us with unflinching starkness how evil and dangerous sin is and how pure the law and love of God are. When you show kids Jesus you don't soften anything; you sharpen everything.

10. Only the confidence that comes from knowing they surely belong to Jesus will let your kids dare to face the full demands of God's law. The best thing of all about Jesus and God's law is that *he kept it*. Joined to him, we are eternally safe. Without this confidence, your kids will reinterpret God's rules into something less rigorous so that they seem manageable. They will always avoid certain demands of God unless they are confident enough in Christ to face them, unafraid of condemnation even though they know progress in fighting them might be painfully slow.

11. Knowing grace lets your kids get serious about God's commands without falling into despair. If you fail to teach grace you'll have to be very careful not to push your kids too hard to obey, because they'll easily get either discouraged or proud. But when they're already confident of God's grace, then you can be much *more forceful* in urging them to obey. You have less worry that even hard teaching about obedience will lead to despair or self-righteousness.

12. Knowing grace makes your kids humble. Grace teaches them that all they have they owe to God. Grace-soaked kids become humble kids, and humble people are happy to obey.

13. Knowing grace makes your kids confident. A life founded on how good they manage to be leads to feelings of guilt and weak self-image, but a life founded on being graciously joined to Jesus leads to the strongest possible self-image: that of being "in Christ." Kids who have Christ as their self-image want to live like him—and confidently trust him to help them do it.

14. Knowing grace leads your kids to worship. Christian worship is a response to who Jesus is and all he's done for us, and doing God's will is an act of "spiritual worship" (Romans 12:1–2). Grace-filled kids don't rejoice in their behavior as much as they rejoice in Jesus—and behave as an overflow of that worship.

15. God means for his kindness to motivate obedience. In Romans, Paul directly addresses the possibility that some people might presume God's forgiveness comes easily and therefore take their sin lightly. But he doesn't say that the solution is to stop teaching grace. Instead, he explains that grace is designed to have the opposite effect: "Do you presume on the riches of his kindness and forbearance and patience, not knowing that God's kindness is meant to lead you to repentance?" (Romans 2:4). God's kindness, when properly understood, leads to repentance. Your kids will see how richly his love has reached down to them—with the compassion of the cross—and be compelled to hate sin like he does.

By now, you've probably noticed that all of these points apply to you too. As *you* look to Jesus and rest in his grace, you become not just a gospel-centered parent but a God-centered person. We hope these studies have helped you along that path, trusting the Savior to bring you ever closer to his side.

LEADER'S NOTES

The Gospel-Centered Parent small group study is designed to help parents live out their faith in Jesus in their family life. All parents know that this is a challenging task, but with God nothing is impossible! He will help us do all that he has called us to do as parents—live by faith in front of our children, share our faith with them, and call them to faith. As the leader of the group, you will have the added privilege of going over the material twice—once before you lead the group, and then in the group. By God's grace, the gospel truths you are talking about with your group will also go deep in your own life and the life of your family.

Each lesson is designed to take a little more than an hour to complete. If your group has more time available, you can simply spend a little longer in the Discussion and Exercise sections. It will be easy for your discussions to last longer than an hour, so plan accordingly and be sure to honor the time commitment that your group has made.

Each group member should receive his or her own resource, so that they can take part in the readings and exercises. There is no outside work required by the study, but it may be that your group will want to think, pray, and go over the questions and exercises at home.

All you need to lead your small group is contained in the content and the leader's notes and suggested answers below. The one thing you *can* do for your group is to take the lead in sharing your own parenting struggles and how you are being challenged, comforted, and encouraged by what you are learning about the gospel applied to parenting. And don't forget to pray with and for your group! The Spirit helps us as we ask. Finally, enjoy watching as God works in his people (including you!).

LESSON 1: UNLESS THE LORD BUILDS THE HOUSE

BIBLE CONVERSATION

In Psalm 127, Solomon writes about safety and prosperity for a household and its community. The psalm deals with a question many of us parents often ask ourselves: *will my family be all right?* **Read all of Psalm 127.** (Have someone in the group read the psalm aloud.)

> (1) Even in tasks like bricklaying and keeping watch, where the skill and diligence of the worker would seem critical, what is the true source of a family's success?

Make sure participants see that God alone gives success. All other efforts are in vain without his blessing. NOTE: This does not mean parents may be lazy or neglectful, but rather that their work as parents is a trusting sort of work that rests in God's goodness. A parent's main work is to turn to God and trust him daily, even in the mundane, ordinary tasks of parenting.

> (2) Long ago, a theologian summarized Psalm 127 by writing, "The order of the home and its success are maintained solely by the blessing of God—not by the policy, diligence and wisdom of men."[4] What besides God are you most tempted to trust for your family's success? Is it your *policies*, your *diligence*, or your *wisdom*? Share an example.

Share actual examples and stories from parenting adventures.

> (3) Starting from the descriptions in verse 2, how might the temperament of a parent who trusts God differ from a must-do-it-myself parent?

Self-trusting parents wear themselves out with worry and perfectionism. This may lead to:

---

[4] John Calvin, *Commentary on Psalms*, trans. James Anderson. http://www.ccel.org/ccel/calvin/calcom12.xi.html.

- Over-protection and controlling behavior
- Anger and blaming
- Disengagement ("Because I might fail, I resist getting involved.")
- Fear and restlessness
- Discontent

Trusting parents work at parenting with a confidence and ease-of-mind that lets them engage the task, even though they often fail, and still sleep at night.

(4) Having many children might seem only to multiply a parent's frustrations. Why do you think Solomon can instead call many children a blessing? How might the frustrations that come with even one child be more manageable when we trust that "the Lord builds the house"?

Parents who believe that God builds the house aren't worn down by the daily frustrations of raising children. They know they don't have to fix everything or get it all right; that's God's job. And they realize their reputation is not on the line; God's is.

DISCUSSION

(5) What parts of Rose Marie's early parenting sound familiar when you think of your own family?

Share personal examples.

(6) How might your parenting be different if you trusted more in God to build your house? What might you *do* (or stop doing) to practice faith in him?

The relationship between "faith" and "doing" can be tricky. But certain kinds of doing are inherently trusting and faith-filled. Examples might include: praying more, acknowledging sin, telling children about Jesus instead of just enforcing rules, or thanking God for his love. These are some of the many ways to rely, moment-by-moment, on the grace of Jesus and his death for us.

(7) Why is it so important for parents to deeply believe (not just know as a point of doctrine) that they are completely forgiven in Jesus?

Good points might include:

- Knowing forgiveness frees parents from performance anxiety or from "beating themselves up" over their parenting, as they learn instead to rest in grace.
- Knowing forgiveness makes parents humble, which helps them put aside anger, blaming, and discontent.
- Knowing forgiveness lets parents teach their children about Jesus, from the heart, rather than mostly nagging them about behavior.

NOTE: *There are many good points that could be made here. It is not necessary to bring up every good answer (and it would take way too long!). Let this question whet your appetite for more gospel-believing blessings to consider in the lessons ahead.*

EXERCISE

Where the exercise is convicting, make sure it leads to prayer, not self-loathing or defensiveness. Believers have access to a Father who is ready to help, and praying is one of the chief signs that a parent is growing in gospel-centeredness.

LESSON 2: THE PARENT AS THE CHIEF REPENTER

BIBLE CONVERSATION

Let's learn about repentance from Psalm 51. The psalm is King David's prayer after he was caught in particularly evil sin; committing adultery with the wife of one of his most loyal soldiers and arranging the man's death to cover it up.

(1) **Read verses 1–6.** David's repentance includes acknowledging the full ugliness of his sin. How is it more than just a one-time mistake? How is the sin more than an outward act? How is the sin more than just hurting his fellow man?

David does not simply acknowledge that he broke God's law; he confesses that he is a sinful person. His sinful heart led him to commit sinful actions. And his sin is not just a way that he hurt some people; it is a personal affront to God: "against you [God], you only, have I sinned" (v. 4). It's usually rather easy for us to admit "mistakes" but harder to confess that we loved doing them. It's easy to say "I'm sorry I hurt you" but harder to say "I was rebellious toward God." The depth of David's confession is part of what makes this an example of full, robust repentance.

(2) **Read verses 7–12.** Would you say David's repentance is about trying hard to do better or about turning to God and trusting his mercy? Besides forgiveness, what more does David ask from God?

Sorrow is more important in repentance than is determining to try harder. Since repentance means turning to God, it is about God having his way in us rather than about us proving ourselves to him. We *receive* from him forgiveness, restoration, and help to change how we live. David longs for all of this; not just a legal declaration of "not guilty," but also the restoration of his relationship with God and the ongoing work of the Holy Spirit in his life. Repentance works healing in all these ways.

(3) **Read verses 13–17.** How will David's repentance in turn help others to repent? What will they notice about David when they see his repentance?

David's repentance makes him able to teach others. It makes him a humble person who's able to praise and worship God with a genuine joy that will be infectious. The application to our parenting is important:

when we freely confess sin and weakness we are able to live among our children as genuine worshipers and effective teachers, inviting them also to live out the gospel in their own lives.

DISCUSSION AND EXERCISE

Keep in mind the fact that, as with all family idols, a family's how-to-be-good-people code may consist of things that are outwardly godly—and good things to do! But they become sinful and dangerous when they take the place of the most important thing, Jesus. Such "good" things are often the hardest idols to set aside because we've convinced ourselves that by doing them, rather than by faith in Jesus, we are a righteous family.

LESSON 3: TEACHING YOUR CHILD "ON THE WAY"

BIBLE CONVERSATION

The book of Deuteronomy is a collection of instructions for God's people. These instructions were given after God had rescued the people from Egypt and was about to bring them into the Promised Land. Chapter 6 is one of the most famous passages in the Old Testament; a summary of what life with God in the land he is giving should look like. **Read Deuteronomy 6:4–12.** (Have someone in the group read the passage aloud.)

(1) Try to describe in a single word or two what this passage says devotion to God should be like. What are some words you might choose?

Good choices might include: steadfast, single-minded, loving, whole, constant, diligent, all-encompassing, grateful, remembering.

(2) To love God *with all your heart* is a tall order. What in this passage helps believers keep God's Word on their hearts?

There are two general helps in this passage:

1. Constant God-focused habits like talking about God throughout the day, and daily reminders like laws posted on the gate, help keep God in mind.
2. Being careful not to forget all of God's goodness in how he's worked salvation (v. 12) keeps the heart focused on him.

(3) Let's think about our own lives. What routines or events help you to think about God as you go through a typical day?

Be careful here not to expect the same level of personal/family devotions or other godly habits from every participant. Believers have both different routines and different levels of maturity, and outward habits don't always indicate mature faith anyway. Our desire is not to compare ourselves with each other, but for all to grow.

(4) What unearned blessings has God given you that you need to be sure not to forget, so that your heart stays tuned toward him?

The many blessings of our own salvation (like forgiveness, deliverance from sin, our status as children of God, daily care from God, fellowship with God and believers, the hope of an eternal home, etc.) may be among the blessings that come to mind. Many of them parallel the blessings listed in the passage, as God intended.

DISCUSSION AND EXERCISE

Throughout the discussion and the exercise there are no right and wrong answers. Help each participant to feel open to share by avoiding pronouncements about who's doing a good job and who isn't. We *all* need to grow.

LESSON 4: DISCIPLINE BY FAITH, NOT FRUSTRATION

BIBLE CONVERSATION

Near the end of Ephesians, the book is about relationships within the home in light of our submission to God. Read the part about children and parents from **Ephesians 6:1–4**. (Have someone read the passage aloud.)

(1) What do you think it means for children to obey their parents "in the Lord"?

Children's obedience to their parents is connected to their life with God, in Christ. Ideally, it should flow from their desire to obey God. It's also a way they serve and honor God. Many kids think having to obey their parents is childish or demeaning, but if they obey "in the Lord" the opposite is true. Obeying and honoring their parents is a concrete way for children to honor God, which is the most mature and noble behavior imaginable. Even the littlest kids can follow God with great splendor—simply by obeying their parents. This should give parents a lot of confidence that it is right and good for them to teach their child to obey.

(2) What are some things that will first have to be true of our parenting if our children are to obey "in the Lord" and because of their hope in God's promises?

Our children will have to learn from us about the Lord and about his promises. To pick up an in-the-Lord mindset, it's also likely that they will have to see us trusting God and living out of his promises daily.

(3) What are the two instructions to fathers? (Note that Paul is addressing only fathers because they would have been responsible for discipline, but his directive applies to both moms and dads.) Give an example of how a parent might do both at the same time.

Fathers are instructed (1) not to provoke their children, and (2) to bring them up in the discipline and instruction of the Lord. An example might be correcting a disobedient child, but doing so not in a way that shames the child but rather in a way that points him to Jesus as part of the correction.

These difficult commands are followed by an instruction to "be strong in the Lord and in the strength of his might" (v. 10). **Have someone read Ephesians 6:14–18.**

(4) The difficult task of parenting is done by taking up God's armor: truth, righteousness, the gospel, faith, salvation, the Word of God, and constant prayer. In a few words, summarize how this affects the way we parent our children.

Possible answers include: We parent in God's power, not our own. Parenting means constant trusting and reliance on God. Our confidence comes from God's goodness to us, not our own abilities. We must believe the gospel to be godly parents.

DISCUSSION

(5) The article says, "Discipline is hard because we do have to correct our children when they sin, but sometimes our own sins muddle the process." Which of your sins most tend to get in the way when you discipline your children?

There is a wide range of possible answers. Not all participants will be like the author of the article. Some will get angry, selfishly demand respect and order, insist on winning for the sake of their own reputation, etc. Others may withdraw from their children, either to protect their reputation when discipline gets risky or out of other misplaced priorities. Some parents might be afraid to discipline because they were corrected in anger as children.

(6) Give an example of how being "secure in the undeserved love of our Father" might make you humble when you correct your child.

Why might it also give you courage to engage tough cases rather than withdrawing?

A deep appreciation of our sinfulness and God's love to us in spite of it makes us humble. It helps us to sympathize with a disobedient child even as we lovingly discipline that child. The security we feel as dearly loved children of our Father helps us overcome the fears that might keep us from enforcing needed discipline. Even though our adventures in discipline might not go as we hope, and our parenting failures might be revealed, we dare to engage the task. We can handle potential failure because our joy comes from Jesus, not from being perfect parents. And we have great confidence that God can use even our bumbling and our weakness to work repentance in our children.

EXERCISE

Try to keep the discussion from becoming too negative. Avoid comparisons with each other, focusing instead on growth for everyone and on the great hope we have when we trust God.

LESSON 5: PARENTING THROUGH PRAYER

BIBLE CONVERSATION

Prayer is at the core of faith in God, so the Bible says much about it. Let's look at a few passages that tell us some prayer basics.

(1) **Read Psalm 145:18–19.** According to these verses, what is God's response to prayer? List some of his qualities.

He is near to those who pray. He fulfills their desires. He hears their cries. He saves them. Notice how by our prayers God is not demanding from us something he needs, but rather is eager to provide for us what we need.

(2) **Read Philippians 4:6–7.** What qualities are found in a believer who prays? List these also.

When we pray we enjoy release from anxiety and the peace of God. We are full of thanksgiving and know that our security is in Christ, not in our own abilities or anything the world promises.

(3) James warns that when we pray selfishly instead of surrendering to God's will, we don't get what we ask. "You ask and do not receive, because you ask wrongly, to spend it on your passions. . . . Humble yourselves before the Lord, and he will exalt you" (James 4:3, 10). It's hard to stay godly-minded in prayer, but **read Romans 8:26–28.** What help do we have when we struggle to pray as we ought? What assurance do we have that God will use even our broken prayers for our good?

The Holy Spirit helps us to pray godly prayers, which will surely be answered "yes." Many believers are familiar with the promise of verse 28, that "all things work together for good," but not many realize that this assurance is about prayer. We can be confident when we pray, sure that God will answer our prayers in ways that are good for us—especially helping us to become more like Jesus (v. 29).

DISCUSSION AND EXERCISE

The prayers suggested in the exercise are only the start of the possible prayers that flow from the Lord's Prayer. Here are some ways to surrender children to God in prayer.

Our Father in heaven

- Thank God that he is the true, best Father of your children whom you may call on for wise and kind care.
- Thank God that he is *your* loving Father too, and ask him to give you the assurance that you are loved by him no matter how successful or unsuccessful your parenting seems to be.
- Ask God to discipline your children well, teaching them to love and follow him.

Hallowed be your name.

- Ask your Father to help your children honor his name in how they behave.
- Praise your Father for his perfect holiness and love.

Your kingdom come. Your will be done, on earth as it is in heaven.

- Pray for your Father to accomplish his purposes through your children.
- Pray for the Spirit to guide and correct your own longings for your children so that they line up with God's purposes (Romans 8:26–27).
- Pray for your Father's help as your family serves his kingdom in specific ways.
- Ask the Spirit to show you and your children ways to do God's will and serve his kingdom.
- Surrender your children to your Father. Confess that you cannot fully see his purposes or the end of your children's lives, so pray that *his* will, not yours, be done in them.

Give us this day our daily bread.

- Pray for specific needs of your children: physical, emotional and spiritual.
- Pray that your Father, who knows every need, would withhold no good thing from your children (Psalm 84:11).

Forgive us our debts, as we also have forgiven our debtors.

- Pray for your relationship with your children: that you and they would be quick to ask and grant forgiveness with each other.
- Confess your own parenting sins and ask your Father to forgive you.
- Ask your Father to grant faith and repentance, leading to eternal forgiveness, to your children.

Lead us not into temptation.

- Ask your Father to give your children strength to resist specific temptations.
- Pray that no temptations would overwhelm your children, but that they would see their sin and be willing to repent.
- Pray for help in protecting your children from the seductions of the world.

Deliver us from evil.

- Pray that your Father would protect your children from the evils of the world, the flesh, and the devil.
- Pray that the Spirit would change your children's hearts, giving them a desire to forsake sin and to truly trust Jesus—not just try harder—for forgiveness and victory over sin.

Yours is the kingdom, and the power, and the glory, forever. Amen.

- Thank God that he is not only your Father, but also Lord and King—powerful and glorious.
- Praise Jesus for his kingdom of glory where weak people are exalted and dying to self brings life.
- Thank your Father that he has the power to carry out what you have prayed for your children.
- Say "amen" with your heart, agreeing with the Spirit in your prayer.

LESSON 6: WHEN YOUR CHILD DISAPPOINTS YOU

BIBLE CONVERSATION

The prophet Hosea told how God loved his people from the time they were an infant nation, saving them out of Egypt and providing every good thing, only to have those people turn their backs on him. **Read Hosea 11:1–4.**

(1) What imagery does God use to describe himself as a Father? What fatherly love and care has he given?

God has loved the people and saved them from Egypt. The imagery he uses reminds us of some of the most tender fatherly behavior we know: teaching a child to walk, holding the child, and bending down to feed the child. God has not been a harsh Father, but has led his people "with bands of love," in a gentle manner that ought to make them loving toward him in return.

(2) How did the people respond to God's fatherly love?

They kept worshiping idols instead of honoring their Father; in fact, the more he pursued them the more they rejected him in return. This is not a one-time sin. It is a pattern of ongoing betrayal and failure to acknowledge God's goodness.

(3) God was angry with the people and determined to apply hard consequences, but did not destroy them. **Read verses 8–9.** What is it about God that keeps him from destroying the wayward people?

God's heart stops him from destroying the people. He is by nature compassionate and tender. Unlike us, his compassion never fails.

(4) If God's approach to his children is a model for us, how might we deal with our children when they disappoint us?

We can remember to act out of love, with compassion, being careful not to destroy our children or our relationship with them by our anger. Some anger is to be expected (the Bible speaks of God getting angry too). But our desire is to control our anger so that it does not become destructive, and to temper it with humility, knowing that we ourselves deserve God's anger but he has shown us great kindness.

DISCUSSION

The article mentioned several emotions that tend to well up in us when our children make bad choices that hurt themselves or us: anger, fear, sadness, discouragement, guilt, and an urge to assign blame. Which ones most fit the way you tend to respond?

Although sin and selfishness are often elements in our emotional responses, not every emotional response is wrong. Rather than criticize each other or "beat ourselves up" for our emotions, take an approach of being honest about emotions and turning to God with them, as often happens in the Psalms.

Have your responses tended to be attempts to manipulate your child, or have you turned in faith to God? Give some examples.

The article says, "It's good to remember that our perfect heavenly Father also has wayward children." How might remembering this help us as we parent our own wayward children?

Possible answers include:

- It keeps us humble and compassionate. We know that we too have disappointed our Father and need his kindness and forgiveness, not just his rebuke.
- It makes us hopeful that God will not give up on our children. Wayward kids are his "specialty"; he loves to bring children back home. He has already done so much to save so many! This gives us a good reason to be hopeful and to spend much time in prayer for our children.
- It shows us how much God cares. Jesus knows what it feels like to have wayward children. He is not blaming us parents, but rather is with us to comfort us.

EXERCISE

It will be especially helpful if participants note how the suggestions in the exercise differ from what usually happens between them and their children. Consider how conflicts might have a different resolution if some of the suggestions were implemented. NOTE: The objection may be raised that sometimes anger is appropriate. This is true. But our anger is usually mixed with selfish pride, and so it is good to be wary of anger and to closely examine our hearts whenever we get angry.

LESSON 7: ADVENTURES IN KINGDOM WORK

BIBLE CONVERSATION

(1) Jesus inaugurated his kingdom during his ministry on earth. **Read Matthew 9:35–38.** List the various aspects of his kingdom work. How might you generally describe the work?

Jesus taught people and proclaimed the gospel to them. He also helped them with physical needs, both medical ones and other afflictions. Ways to describe the work might include the following:

- It involves going out to people, finding and meeting them where they live.
- It includes both speaking words of hope and truth and doing deeds of mercy and kindness.
- It is motivated by compassion for those who have not been taught or cared for well.
- It is a harvest; a glad and necessary time of bringing people into God's kingdom care, much like a farmer eagerly brings ready crops into his barn.

(2) Jesus says he is looking for others to join in these aspects of his work. How might you describe the type of workers needed? What spiritual characteristics will they share with Jesus?

Like Jesus, the workers are willing to go out and work. They are full of compassion for others, especially when they see others' needs. They are also people of prayer, trusting God to provide what is needed for the harvest. They are not working on their own; they are sent by the Lord of the harvest.

(3) How might this kingdom work compare to other work we typically do in the world?

- One great joy of kingdom work is that it focuses our attention away from ourselves—both away from our own needs and "comfort zone" and away from our own abilities to perform. The work Jesus describes involves going out to meet people on their "turf" and showing compassion to them in whatever way they need. It also involves leaning on God in prayer, rather than trusting our own abilities, so that the Lord is the one who sends us and accomplishes his harvest. Kingdom work is big, fulfilling work because it is God's work.

- Another joy of kingdom work is that is it urgent work. The fields are ready for harvest and the Lord is eager to see his kingdom expand on earth. To be involved in the culmination of his plan for the world is a great adventure. As a farmer at harvest time thrills to see the fruition of months of fieldwork and waiting, so we in this age are stirred to join the Lord's harvest.

(4) **Read Matthew 6:19–21.** How does this teaching from Jesus add to the appeal of service in his kingdom?

Kingdom work helps us and our children to set our priorities right. It trains us to hope in the things of heaven rather than the comforts of earth, and in the people and activities that move God's heart rather than in selfish desires.

DISCUSSION AND EXERCISE

There are no right and wrong answers, and no firm commitment to do anything at this point other than consider, dream, and pray—no pressure!

LESSON 8: WALKING WITH YOUR FAMILY THROUGH SUFFERING

BIBLE CONVERSATION

John 9 tells the story of Jesus's encounter with a man born blind and his parents. Have someone **read John 9:1–7** aloud.

(1) The blind man and his parents must have suffered much. According to Jesus, what was the purpose behind that suffering?

The blindness was "that the works of God might be displayed in him" (John 9:3). The man was blind so that Jesus could heal him and show himself to be the light of the world (and also for the loving purpose of bringing the man to faith—but that comes later).

(2) How does Jesus's answer make you feel about suffering? What's encouraging about his answer? Is there anything that feels insensitive or incomplete about it?

It may feel encouraging that:

- God has a plan in suffering.
- Those who suffer greatly may be most suited to display God's glory and witness to his saving works and compassion.
- Suffering is not necessarily a punishment, and when our children suffer it isn't necessarily our fault. God isn't getting back at us; he's teaching and loving us.

It may feel incomplete or insensitive because:

- Jesus seems at this point to have a philosophical answer rather than a compassionate one.
- Without the healing that accompanies it, Jesus's answer alone would not be very helpful to the blind man.

As the story in John 9 progresses, the blind man tells what Jesus did for him, and Jesus's enemies cast the blind man out of the synagogue (like being expelled from church) for his testimony. **Read John 9:35–39** to see what Jesus did then.

(3) What evidence do you see of Jesus's compassion for the blind man—both while the man was still blind and later when he was persecuted? List several things that Jesus did for him, both in the latter part of the story and at the beginning.

Possible answers include:

- Jesus affirmed the blind man's worth by caring for him and asserting that no one was to blame for his condition.
- Jesus got close and personal with him, using touch and spit.
- Jesus gave him an opportunity to practice faith by following the instructions to wash.
- Jesus healed him.
- Jesus followed up, learning about how the man was cast out of the synagogue.
- When he heard how the man was treated, Jesus searched for him and found him.
- Jesus told the man about himself and helped him to believe.
- Jesus put to rest any lingering suspicions that the blindness was the fault of the man or his parents or that they should feel guilty, focusing instead on the guilt of the Pharisees.

(4) Why does it matter that this account both teaches the truth that the family's suffering was for good and also shows Jesus's compassion and care? (The man came to faith! Others saw a sign of Jesus's power and compassion. Some who saw were challenged about their own blindness.)

It is not enough to know that God controls all things and has a good plan even in times of suffering. We also need the comfort of knowing that he is tuned to hear our groaning and cares greatly (Exodus 2:24). Likewise, it is not enough just to know that God cares. We need to know that the same Savior who weeps with us also has the power and determination to one day eliminate all our tears (Revelation 7:17).

DISCUSSION

The article mentions three things to teach our children about suffering:

- God is with us through suffering but won't rescue us from suffering until heaven.
- We cannot fully imagine what wonders God has in store for us.
- The promises and friendship of Jesus are far better than an easy life.

(5) What other truths about Jesus and the gospel do you think are particularly important to teach our children as we walk with them through suffering?

If Christ is in the center of our lives, our thoughts will surely turn to him in times of suffering, so there are many good answers. Some already noted in this lesson include:

- Jesus is compassionate toward those who are suffering.
- Jesus himself suffered greatly in order to rescue us from the greatest suffering of all (and one day from all suffering).
- Suffering is an opportunity to grow in faith and to gain confidence that our faith is legitimate.
- The Christian life isn't about avoiding suffering, but rather about living fully and faithfully in the midst of suffering.
- Suffering helps us to draw closer to God. We can go to him in every kind of suffering, sure that he cares.
- Jesus understands our suffering.
- In Jesus, we have great hope even though we suffer now.
- God is in charge even though he allows some suffering. Jesus is King over all, even over evil!
- Suffering reminds us that God's work is not finished and we have not yet arrived at our final home. It trains us to keep looking ahead and "lay up treasures in heaven" (Matthew 6:19–21).
- God may be using your suffering not only to bless you, but also to help you be a blessing to others.

(6) If you can, share an example of a truth about Jesus and the gospel that was helpful to your family during a time of suffering.

(7) Think about what you know of how Jesus approached his own suffering and death. (Did he feel it strongly or suppress it? How did he engage others? How did he engage God?) What can you learn from him about how to act when suffering comes?

Jesus was not afraid to show that he was suffering. He sweated in Gethsemane and cried out on the cross. Yet he kept caring for others (his disciples, his mother, and even the soldiers who were responsible for his suffering), and he kept praying to his heavenly Father. The Gospels suggest that some of Jesus's deepest prayer and most important moments with his disciples came during the final days before his death when he was suffering the most. We can do the same—draw close to God and share with others during times of suffering.

EXERCISE

The fear, anger, and other feelings that often accompany suffering are not surprising, and no one should feel scolded for admitting to them. Still, try to see how the gospel ought to produce a measure of hope, compassion, forgiveness, and contentment in us, even in the midst of deep suffering.

LESSON 9: SPIRITUAL WARFARE AND YOUR FAMILY
BIBLE CONVERSATION

(1) Read **1 John 2:15–17**. What is the alternative to loving the things of our heavenly Father? Does this threat come from *outside* of us or from the *inside*? Explain.

The alternative to love of the Father is love of the world. In one sense these are things outside of us. "The world" is a system of life in which the things we see and possess are regarded as our chief loves, even though those are lesser things that are passing away. But in another sense the struggle is very much an internal one. It is about our desires, our pride, and what we value.

(2) Now read Paul's account of his personal battle with sin from **Romans 7:21–25**. Does this threat come from the outside or from inside of him? Give an example of situation in which you knew what was right and wanted to do right, but still gave in to another inward desire to do what was wrong.

Paul's battle is against the sinful nature that remains inside of believers even after they are made alive in Christ. The new life given us by the Spirit enables us to join the fight against sin but does not yet free us from sin's influence.

> (3) The temptation to sin is particularly dangerous because it has a personal, scheming force behind it. Read **Ephesians 6:10–17**. Looking at verses 10–12, list some words you might use to describe our adversary.

The devil is described as evil, cosmically powerful, dark, and a spiritual ruler. NOTE: The use of the word "forces" here does not mean the devil is an impersonal force, but rather that he is like an army commander who has many evil forces at his disposal.

> (4) Later we'll look in detail at the armor "pieces," but in general, what hope do we have to stand against the devil?

Our hope against the devil is the Lord and his strength; the armor of God.

DISCUSSION

> (5) Ephesians 6 says faith in Christ extinguishes the flaming darts of the evil one. What darts (lies or doubts about God's goodness) has the evil one hurled at you or your children recently? How do they threaten to keep you from living for God?

Share personal examples.

> (6) How does the promise that he who is in us (God) is more powerful than he who is in the world (the devil) affect our daily parenting?

Possible answers include:

- The reminder of God's power ought to make us quick to turn to him with any need.

- We will be humble and prayerful.
- We will not despair even when we see that sin runs deep and solutions seem impossible, but will persevere in our parenting because our confidence is in God's power rather than our own abilities.

EXERCISE

Try to remain focused on the temptation in the case study, not on potential ways to fix the problem that led to the temptation. Growth through repentance and by resisting temptation is often a big reason why God brings trials into our lives. Fixing a problem may be far less important than, say, learning to love an enemy. The problem itself might be easily fixed by worldly means, but the temptations and heart issues that accompany it will require the armor of God.

In discussing the armor, it is not necessary to consider how salvation may be more like a helmet than like shoes, and so on. The main point is simply that these aspects of the gospel are protection and help in the battle to resist sin. For example:

- The TRUTH that Jesus has overcome the world may keep us from pursuing vengeance when it looks like others are out to get us, or the TRUTH that our inheritance is in heaven may keep us from idolizing worldly success and enjoyments—and getting angry at anyone who keeps us from them.
- The GOSPEL OF PEACE may help us want others to come to know that peace too, so that we respond to them (even when they sin against us!) in ways that make peace and winsomely share our hope in Jesus.
- Our SALVATION may remind us that we too are big sinners deserving judgment who've been shown abundant grace, so that we become humble and gracious in dealing with others.
- FAITH may help us see that God's plans are good even when we face severe disappointments. We become thankful in every circumstance (1 Thessalonians 5:18) rather than resentful.

LESSON 10: PERSEVERANCE AND HOPE
BIBLE CONVERSATION

Psalm 13 is a common kind of psalm called a *lament*. A lament expresses the feelings that come when life seems to be going very wrong. This psalm of David has three parts: it starts in anguish, progresses through prayer, and ends in hope. Have someone **read all of Psalm 13**.

> (1) *Part 1: Anguish.* Describe how David's troubles feel to him in verses 1 and 2. We don't know what David's troubles were at this time, but think of a few parenting troubles that might lead a mom or dad to have the same kind of feelings.

David feels as if God has forgotten him and is "hiding his face" from him—that is, he feels as if God no longer notices him or shows him favor. His sorrow is the sort that does not go away, but is with him all the time. David also feels as if his enemies are receiving more favor than he is—we might say David feels like a "loser." All of these feelings are familiar to parents who've been through trying ordeals involving their children.

> (2) *Part 2: Prayer.* When life has so many problems, our only relief is to turn to God. In verse 3, what might David mean when he asks the Lord to light up his eyes?

David's concern is not necessarily about physical death; it may also be a request for faith. One thing that happens to us when we have many troubles is that it becomes difficult to see what is true and good—to see the light. In such situations, one of the best things we can pray for is faith, asking God to help us see beyond our current troubles and believe that he is good.

> (3) *Part 3: Hope.* Describe the change that takes place in David at the end of the psalm, after he has brought his troubles to God. What's different inside of him?

David becomes ready to worship. He moves from despair to trust and from overwhelming sadness to a life that includes inward joy. Rather than feeling forgotten by God, David remembers God's love and the ways God has been generous to him. He is so sure of salvation that he is prepared to rejoice in it already. All of this is despite the fact that the psalm gives no indication that David's troubles have ended or that he has received any answer to his cry of "how long?"—he knows only that God surely will answer in love.

DISCUSSION AND EXERCISE

It's important not to leave this study feeling that now you know how to fix your family problems. Rather, try to leave feeling that now you need more than ever to trust God in all things and pray without ceasing. If participants leave encouraged to do that, this study will have been a great success!

mission
propelled by good news

At Serge we believe that mission begins through the gospel of Jesus Christ bringing God's grace into the lives of believers. This good news also sustains and empowers us to cross nations and cultures to bring the gospel of grace to those whom God is calling to himself.

As a cross-denominational, reformed, sending agency with more than 200 missionaries and 25 teams in 5 continents, we are always looking for people who are ready to take the next step in sharing Christ, through:

- **Short-term Teams**: One- to two-week trips oriented around serving overseas ministries while equipping the local church for mission

- **Internships:** Eight-week to nine-month opportunities to learn about missions through serving with our overseas ministry teams

- **Apprenticeships:** Intensive 12–24 month training and ministry opportunities for those discerning their call to cross-cultural ministry

- **Career:** One- to five-year appointments designed to nurture you for a lifetime of ministry

 Grace at the Fray

Visit us online at: serge.org/mission

www.newgrowthpress.com

spiritual renewal resources for you

Disciples who are motivated and empowered by grace to reach out to a broken world are handmade, not mass-produced. Serge intentionally grows disciples through curriculum, discipleship experiences, and training programs.

Resources for Every Stage of Growth

Serge offers grace-based, gospel-centered studies for every stage of the Christian journey. Every level of our materials focuses on essential aspects of how the Spirit transforms and motivates us through the gospel of Jesus Christ.

- **101**: The Gospel-Centered Series
  Gospel-centered studies on Christian growth, community, work, parenting, and more.
- **201**: The Gospel Transformation Series
  These studies go a step deeper into gospel transformation, involve homework and more in-depth Bible study
- **301**: The Sonship Course and Serge Individual Mentoring

Mentored Sonship

For more than 25 years Serge has been discipling ministry leaders around the world through our Sonship course to help them experience the freedom and joy of having the gospel transform every part of their lives. A personal discipler will help you apply what you are learning to the daily struggles and situations you face, as well as, model what a gospel-centered faith looks and feels like.

Discipler Training Course

Serge's Discipler Training Course helps you gain biblical understanding and practical wisdom you need to disciple others so they experience substantive, lasting growth in their lives. Available for onsite training or via distance learning, our training programs are ideal for ministry leaders, small group leaders or those seeking to grow in their ability to disciple effectively.

 Grace at the Fray   **Find more resources at serge.org**

resources and mentoring for every stage of growth

Every day around the world, Serge teams help people develop and deepen a living, breathing, growing relationship with Jesus. We help people connect with God in ways that are genuinely grace-motivated and increase desire and ability to reach out to others. No matter where you are along the way, we have a series that is right for you.

101: The *Gospel-Centered* Series

Our *Gospel-Centered* series is simple, deep, and transformative. Each *Gospel-Centered* lesson features an easy-to-read article and provides challenging discussion questions and application questions. Best of all, no outside preparation on the part of the participants is needed! They are perfect for small groups, those who are seeking to develop "gospel DNA" in their organizations and leaders, and contexts where people are still wrestling with what it means to follow Jesus.

201: The *Gospel Transformation* Series

Our *Gospel Transformation* studies take the themes introduced in our 101-level materials and expand and deepen them. Designed for those seeking to grow through directly studying Scripture each *Gospel Transformation* lesson helps participants grow in the way they understand and experience God's grace. Ideal for small groups, individuals who are ready for more, and one-on-one mentoring, *Gospel Identity*, *Gospel Growth*, and *Gospel Love* provide substantive material, in easy-to-use, manageable sized studies.

The *Sonship* Course and Individual Mentoring from Serge

Developed for use with our own missionaries and used for over 25 years with thousands of Christian leaders in every corner of the world, Sonship sets the standard for whole-person, life transformation through the gospel. Designed to be used with a mentor, or in groups ready for a high investment with each other, each lesson focuses on the type of "inductive heart study" that brings about change from the inside out.

 Grace at the Fray

Visit us online at serge.org

www.newgrowthpress.com